Contents

Russian Tea Cakes

Prep: 15 mins **Cook:** 15 mins **Total:** 30 mins **Servings:** 14 **Yield:** 28 to 32 cookies

Ingredients

- 1 cup unsalted butter, room temperature
- 1 ⅓ cups confectioners' sugar, divided
- 1 cup finely chopped toasted walnuts
- ⅛ teaspoon salt
- 1 teaspoon vanilla extract
- 2 cups all-purpose flour
- 2 tablespoons all-purpose flour
- 1 cup confectioners' sugar for dusting, or more as needed

Directions

Step 1

Preheat oven to 350 degrees F (175 degrees C). Arrange rack in center position of oven.

Step 2

Place butter, 1/3 cup packed powdered sugar, walnuts, salt, and vanilla in a bowl. Top with the flour. Mix with your clean hands until the dough starts to clump up. Keep mixing by hand until all the flour and clumps of butter are evenly mixed into the dough and it can be easily formed into balls.

Step 3

Scoop out dough and roll by hand into uniformly round balls, just slightly larger than 1 inch. Place on a rimmed baking sheet lined with a silicone baking mat about 2 inches apart.

Step 4

Bake in preheated oven until lightly golden, 15 to 25 minutes depending on the size of the cookies.

Step 5

Let cool exactly 5 minutes then roll in remaining 1 cup confectioners' sugar. Let cookies cool completely and toss them again in the confectioners' sugar.

Nutrition Facts

Per Serving:

320.7 calories; protein 3.4g 7% DV; carbohydrates 36.1g 12% DV; fat 18.8g 29% DV; cholesterol 34.9mg 12% DV; sodium 23.3mg 1% DV.

Hedgehog Cookies

Prep: 1 hr **Cook:** 10 mins **Additional:** 2 hrs **Total:** 3 hrs 10 mins **Servings:** 24 **Yield:** 4 dozen cookies

Ingredients

- 4 cups all-purpose flour
- ¾ teaspoon baking powder
- ½ teaspoon baking soda
- ½ teaspoon salt
- 1 ¼ cups white sugar
- 1 cup butter-flavored shortening
- ¼ cup corn syrup
- 2 large eggs eggs
- 1 tablespoon vanilla extract
- 1 cup pecans
- 1 cup chocolate chips

Directions

Step 1

Mix flour, baking powder, baking soda, and salt in a bowl. Whisk sugar, shortening, corn syrup, eggs, and vanilla extract in a separate bowl. Stir sugar mixture into flour mixture until just combined. Refrigerate dough until chilled, 30 minutes to 1 hour.

Step 2

Preheat oven to 350 degrees F (175 degrees C).

Step 3

Scoop cookie dough using a cookie scoop or 1 tablespoon so all the cookies are uniform; shape dough into teardrop-shaped cookies. Flatten the pointed side of each cookie to form the 'face'. Arrange cookies on baking sheets.

Step 4

Bake in the preheated oven until golden, 10 to 12 minutes. Cool on the baking sheets for 10 minutes before removing to cool completely on a wire rack.

Step 5

Pulse pecans in a food processor until finely chopped; transfer to a bowl.

Step 6

Melt chocolate chips in the top of a double boiler over simmering water, stirring frequently and scraping down the sides with a rubber spatula to avoid scorching.

Step 7

Dip the top of each cookie in the melted chocolate, spreading to fully coat the 'body' of each hedgehog. Press cookies, chocolate-side down, into the ground pecans forming the 'fur'. Arrange cookies on a sheet of waxed paper to set, about 30 minutes.

Step 8

Transfer the remaining melted chocolate to a piping bag or plastic bag with a corner snipped. Pipe chocolate onto the pointed end of each cookie for eyes and a nose.

Nutrition Facts

Per Serving:

280.1 calories; protein 3.4g 7% DV; carbohydrates 34.2g 11% DV; fat 15.2g 23% DV; cholesterol 15.5mg 5% DV; sodium 99.1mg 4% DV.

Royal Icing II

Prep: 15 mins **Total:** 15 mins **Servings:** 48 **Yield:** 3 cups

Ingredients

- 3 tablespoons meringue powder
- 4 cups sifted confectioners' sugar
- 6 tablespoons water

Directions

Step 1

Beat all ingredients at low speed for 7 to 10 minutes, or until icing forms peaks. Tip: Keep icing covered with a wet kitchen towel at all times. Icing can dry out quickly.

Nutrition Facts

Per Serving:

43.4 calories; protein 0.2g; carbohydrates 10.8g 4% DV; fatg; cholesterolmg; sodium 2.7mg.

Russian Tea Cakes I

Prep: 20 mins **Cook:** 12 mins **Additional:** 3 mins **Total:** 35 mins **Servings:** 36 **Yield:** 3 dozen

Ingredients

- 1 cup butter
- 1 teaspoon vanilla extract
- 6 tablespoons confectioners' sugar
- 2 cups all-purpose flour
- 1 cup chopped walnuts
- ⅓ cup confectioners' sugar for decoration

Directions

Step 1

Preheat oven to 350 degrees F (175 degrees C).

Step 2

In a medium bowl, cream butter and vanilla until smooth. Combine the 6 tablespoons confectioners' sugar and flour; stir into the butter mixture until just blended. Mix in the chopped walnuts. Roll dough into 1 inch balls, and place them 2 inches apart on an ungreased cookie sheet.

Step 3

Bake for 12 minutes in the preheated oven. When cool, roll in remaining confectioners' sugar. I also like to roll mine in the sugar a second time.

Nutrition Facts

Per Serving:

101.6 calories; protein 1.3g 3% DV; carbohydrates 8.2g 3% DV; fat 7.3g 11% DV; cholesterol 13.6mg 5% DV; sodium 36.6mg 2% DV.

Chocolate Peppermint Biscotti

Prep: 1 hr **Cook:** 50 mins **Additional:** 1 hr **Total:** 2 hrs 50 mins **Servings:** 32 **Yield:** 32 biscotti

Ingredients

- 2 cups white sugar
- 1 cup butter, softened
- 1 cup unsweetened cocoa powder
- 4 large eggs eggs
- ⅓ cup chocolate liqueur (such as Godiva)
- 2 teaspoons peppermint extract
- 4 ½ cups all-purpose flour
- 4 teaspoons baking powder
- ¾ teaspoon salt
- 1 ⅔ cups mint chocolate chips (such as Hershey's)

- 2 (14 ounce) packages white candy melts (confectioners' coating)
- 6 eaches large peppermint candy canes, crushed

Directions

Step 1

Preheat oven to 350 degrees F (175 degrees C). Line two baking sheets with parchment paper.

Step 2

Beat white sugar, butter, and cocoa powder together with an electric mixer in a large bowl until creamy and smooth. Add eggs, one at a time, beating well after each addition. Mix chocolate liqueur and peppermint extract into the sugar-egg mixture.

Step 3

Combine flour, baking powder, and salt in a separate bowl. Slowly mix flour mixture into sugar-egg mixture until fully incorporated; fold mint chocolate chips into the dough.

Step 4

Divide dough into 4 equal parts and shape into logs. Arrange the logs on the prepared baking sheets.

Step 5

Dip a spatula in water and use it to smooth surface of the logs.

Step 6

Bake biscotti logs in the preheated oven until firm to the touch, 30 to 35 minutes. Cool biscotti logs completely on wire racks.

Step 7

Reduce oven temperature to 300 degrees F (150 degrees C).

Step 8

Cut biscotti logs into 3/4-inch slices and arrange on baking sheets.

Step 9

Bake in the oven until biscotti are dry, about 10 minutes per side. Cool completely on wire racks.

Step 10

Place candy melts in a wide microwave-safe bowl; heat in microwave until melted, about 2 1/2 minutes, stirring every 30 seconds.

Step 11

Dip cooled biscotti in the melted white candy; sprinkle with crushed candy canes.

Nutrition Facts

Per Serving:

385.8 calories; protein 5.2g 11% DV; carbohydrates 54.1g 18% DV; fat 17.3g 27% DV; cholesterol 43.6mg 15% DV; sodium 190.2mg 8% DV.

Chocolate Rum Balls I

Prep: 45 mins **Total:** 45 mins **Servings:** 48 **Yield:** 4 dozen

Ingredients

- 3 ¼ cups crushed vanilla wafers
- ¾ cup confectioners' sugar
- ¼ cup unsweetened cocoa powder

- 1 ½ cups chopped walnuts
- 3 tablespoons light corn syrup
- ½ cup rum

Directions

Step 1

In a large bowl, stir together the crushed vanilla wafers, 3/4 cup confectioners' sugar, cocoa, and nuts. Blend in corn syrup and rum.

Step 2

Shape into 1 inch balls, and roll in additional confectioners' sugar. Store in an airtight container for several days to develop the flavor. Roll again in confectioners' sugar before serving.

Nutrition Facts

Per Serving:

98.8 calories; protein 1.2g 2% DV; carbohydrates 12.3g 4% DV; fat 4.8g 7% DV; cholesterolmg; sodium 38.3mg 2% DV.

Citrus Shortbread Cookies

Prep: 25 mins **Cook:** 10 mins **Additional:** 4 hrs **Total:** 4 hrs 35 mins **Servings:** 24 **Yield:** 2 dozen

Ingredients

- 2 cups all-purpose flour
- ¼ teaspoon baking powder
- ⅛ teaspoon salt
- 1 cup butter, softened
- ¾ cup confectioners' sugar
- 2 teaspoons vanilla extract
- ½ teaspoon almond extract
- 1 tablespoon grated orange zest, or more to taste
- 2 cups sweetened dried cranberries, chopped

Directions

Step 1

Combine flour, baking powder, and salt in a bowl; set aside. Beat the butter and confectioners' sugar with an electric mixer in a large bowl until smooth. Stir in the vanilla and almond extracts and orange zest. Mix in the flour mixture until just incorporated. Fold in the cranberries; mixing just enough to evenly combine.

Step 2

Divide the dough into 2 equal portions, then roll into logs about 7 inches long. Wrap each log in wax paper or plastic wrap, and chill in the refrigerator for at least 4 hours.

Step 3

Preheat an oven to 350 degrees F (175 degrees C).

Step 4

Remove wax paper, and cut the cookie dough into 1/2-inch slices. Arrange the slices on a baking sheet about 1 inch apart.

Step 5

Bake in the preheated oven until firm but not browned, about 10 minutes.

Nutrition Facts

Per Serving:

152.5 calories; protein 1.2g 2% DV; carbohydrates 20.2g 7% DV; fat 7.8g 12% DV; cholesterol 20.3mg 7% DV; sodium 72mg 3% DV.

Crescent Butter Biscuits

Prep: 30 mins **Cook:** 10 mins **Additional:** 1 hr **Total:** 1 hr 40 mins **Servings:** 100 **Yield:** 100 cookies

Ingredients

- 2 ½ cups all-purpose flour
- 1 ¾ cups almond flour
- ¾ cup white sugar
- 1 cup butter
- 3 large egg yolks egg yolks
- 1 tablespoon vanilla sugar, or as needed

Directions

Step 1

Combine all-purpose flour, almond flour, and sugar in a bowl; rub in butter using your fingers until coarse crumbs form. Add egg yolks and work into a smooth dough. Wrap dough in plastic wrap and chill in the refrigerator for 1 hour.

Step 2

Preheat oven to 350 degrees F (175 degrees C). Line a baking sheet with parchment paper.

Step 3

Turn dough onto a floured work surface; roll into long, thin pieces. Cut into 2-inch pieces and shape each piece into a crescent-shape. Place crescents on the prepared baking sheet.

Step 4

Bake in preheated oven until lightly golden, 10 to 15 minutes. Immediately roll the crescents in vanilla sugar while hot. Set aside to cool.

Nutrition Facts

Per Serving:

48.2 calories; protein 0.9g 2% DV; carbohydrates 4.5g 1% DV; fat 3.1g 5% DV; cholesterol 11mg 4% DV; sodium 13.4mg 1% DV.

Best Chocolate Chip Cookies

Prep: 20 mins **Cook:** 10 mins **Additional:** 30 mins **Total:** 1 hr **Servings:** 24 **Yield:** 4 dozen

Ingredients

- 1 cup butter, softened
- 1 cup white sugar
- 1 cup packed brown sugar
- 2 large eggs eggs
- 2 teaspoons vanilla extract
- 1 teaspoon baking soda

- 2 teaspoons hot water
- ½ teaspoon salt
- 3 cups all-purpose flour
- 2 cups semisweet chocolate chips
- 1 cup chopped walnuts

Directions

Step 1

Preheat oven to 350 degrees F (175 degrees C).

Step 2

Cream together the butter, white sugar, and brown sugar until smooth. Beat in the eggs one at a time, then stir in the vanilla. Dissolve baking soda in hot water. Add to batter along with salt. Stir in flour, chocolate chips, and nuts. Drop by large spoonfuls onto ungreased pans.

Step 3

Bake for about 10 minutes in the preheated oven, or until edges are nicely browned.

Nutrition Facts

Per Serving:

297.8 calories; protein 3.6g 7% DV; carbohydrates 38.9g 13% DV; fat 15.6g 24% DV; cholesterol 35.8mg 12% DV; sodium 165.8mg 7% DV.

Easy Sugar Cookies

Prep: 15 mins **Cook:** 10 mins **Total:** 25 mins **Servings:** 48 **Yield:** 4 dozen

Ingredients

- 2 ¾ cups all-purpose flour
- 1 teaspoon baking soda
- ½ teaspoon baking powder
- 1 cup butter, softened

- 1 ½ cups white sugar
- 1 egg
- 1 teaspoon vanilla extract

Directions

Step 1

Preheat oven to 375 degrees F (190 degrees C). In a small bowl, stir together flour, baking soda, and baking powder. Set aside.

Step 2

In a large bowl, cream together the butter and sugar until smooth. Beat in egg and vanilla. Gradually blend in the dry ingredients. Roll rounded teaspoonfuls of dough into balls, and place onto ungreased cookie sheets.

Step 3

Bake 8 to 10 minutes in the preheated oven, or until golden. Let stand on cookie sheet two minutes before removing to cool on wire racks.

Nutrition Facts

Per Serving:

85.9 calories; protein 0.9g 2% DV; carbohydrates 11.7g 4% DV; fat 4g 6% DV; cholesterol 14mg 5% DV; sodium 60.1mg 2% DV.

Best Big, Fat, Chewy Chocolate Chip Cookie

Prep: 10 mins **Cook:** 15 mins **Additional:** 15 mins **Total:** 40 mins **Servings:** 18 **Yield:** 1 1/2 dozen

Ingredients

- 2 cups all-purpose flour
- ½ teaspoon baking soda
- ½ teaspoon salt
- ¾ cup unsalted butter, melted
- 1 cup packed brown sugar
- ½ cup white sugar
- 1 tablespoon vanilla extract
- 1 egg
- 1 egg yolk
- 2 cups semisweet chocolate chips

Directions

Step 1

Preheat the oven to 325 degrees F (165 degrees C). Grease cookie sheets or line with parchment paper.

Step 2

Sift together the flour, baking soda and salt; set aside.

Step 3

In a medium bowl, cream together the melted butter, brown sugar and white sugar until well blended. Beat in the vanilla, egg, and egg yolk until light and creamy. Mix in the sifted ingredients until just blended. Stir in the chocolate chips by hand using a wooden spoon. Drop cookie dough 1/4 cup at a time onto the prepared cookie sheets. Cookies should be about 3 inches apart.

Step 4

Bake for 15 to 17 minutes in the preheated oven, or until the edges are lightly toasted. Cool on baking sheets for a few minutes before transferring to wire racks to cool completely.

Nutrition Facts

Per Serving:

284.7 calories; protein 2.8g 6% DV; carbohydrates 40.1g 13% DV; fat 13.9g 21% DV; cholesterol 42mg 14% DV; sodium 110.7mg 4% DV.

Iced Pumpkin Cookies

Prep: 20 mins **Cook:** 20 mins **Additional:** 40 mins **Total:** 1 hr 20 mins **Servings:** 36 **Yield:** 3 dozen

Ingredients

- 2 ½ cups all-purpose flour
- 1 teaspoon baking powder
- 1 teaspoon baking soda
- 2 teaspoons ground cinnamon
- ½ teaspoon ground nutmeg
- ½ teaspoon ground cloves
- ½ teaspoon salt
- ½ cup butter, softened

- 1 ½ cups white sugar
- 1 cup canned pumpkin puree
- 1 egg
- 1 teaspoon vanilla extract
- 2 cups confectioners' sugar
- 3 tablespoons milk
- 1 tablespoon melted butter
- 1 teaspoon vanilla extract

Directions

Step 1

Preheat oven to 350 degrees F (175 degrees C). Combine flour, baking powder, baking soda, cinnamon, nutmeg, ground cloves, and salt; set aside.

Step 2

In a medium bowl, cream together the 1/2 cup of butter and white sugar. Add pumpkin, egg, and 1 teaspoon vanilla to butter mixture, and beat until creamy. Mix in dry ingredients. Drop on cookie sheet by tablespoonfuls; flatten slightly.

Step 3

Bake for 15 to 20 minutes in the preheated oven. Cool cookies, then drizzle glaze with fork.

Step 4

To Make Glaze: Combine confectioners' sugar, milk, 1 tablespoon melted butter, and 1 teaspoon vanilla. Add milk as needed, to achieve drizzling consistency.

Nutrition Facts

Per Serving:

121.5 calories; protein 1.2g 3% DV; carbohydrates 22.4g 7% DV; fat 3.2g 5% DV; cholesterol 12.9mg 4% DV; sodium 120.5mg 5% DV.

The Best Rolled Sugar Cookies

Prep: 20 mins **Cook:** 8 mins **Additional:** 2 hrs 32 mins **Total:** 3 hrs **Servings:** 60 **Yield:** 5 dozen

Ingredients

- 1 ½ cups butter, softened
- 2 cups white sugar
- 4 large eggs eggs
- 1 teaspoon vanilla extract

- 5 cups all-purpose flour
- 2 teaspoons baking powder
- 1 teaspoon salt

Directions

Step 1

In a large bowl, cream together butter and sugar until smooth. Beat in eggs and vanilla. Stir in the flour, baking powder, and salt. Cover, and chill dough for at least one hour (or overnight).

Step 2

Preheat oven to 400 degrees F (200 degrees C). Roll out dough on floured surface 1/4 to 1/2 inch thick. Cut into shapes with any cookie cutter. Place cookies 1 inch apart on ungreased cookie sheets.

Step 3

Bake 6 to 8 minutes in preheated oven. Cool completely.

Nutrition Facts

Per Serving:

109.5 calories; protein 1.5g 3% DV; carbohydrates 14.7g 5% DV; fat 5g 8% DV; cholesterol 24.6mg 8% DV; sodium 92.6mg 4% DV.

Big Soft Ginger Cookies

Prep: 15 mins **Cook:** 10 mins **Additional:** 25 mins **Total:** 50 mins **Servings:** 24 **Yield:** 2 dozen

Ingredients

- 2 ¼ cups all-purpose flour
- 2 teaspoons ground ginger
- 1 teaspoon baking soda
- ¾ teaspoon ground cinnamon
- ½ teaspoon ground cloves
- ¼ teaspoon salt
- ¾ cup margarine, softened
- 1 cup white sugar
- 1 egg
- 1 tablespoon water
- ¼ cup molasses
- 2 tablespoons white sugar

Directions

Step 1

Preheat oven to 350 degrees F (175 degrees C). Sift together the flour, ginger, baking soda, cinnamon, cloves, and salt. Set aside.

Step 2

In a large bowl, cream together the margarine and 1 cup sugar until light and fluffy. Beat in the egg, then stir in the water and molasses. Gradually stir the sifted ingredients into the molasses mixture. Shape dough into walnut sized balls, and roll them in the remaining 2 tablespoons of sugar. Place the cookies 2 inches apart onto an ungreased cookie sheet, and flatten slightly.

Step 3

Bake for 8 to 10 minutes in the preheated oven. Allow cookies to cool on baking sheet for 5 minutes before removing to a wire rack to cool completely. Store in an airtight container.

Nutrition Facts

Per Serving:

142.8 calories; protein 1.6g 3% DV; carbohydrates 21.1g 7% DV; fat 6g 9% DV; cholesterol 7.8mg 3% DV; sodium 147mg 6% DV.

Macaron (French Macaroon)

Prep: 30 mins **Cook:** 10 mins **Additional:** 1 hr 30 mins **Total:** 2 hrs 10 mins **Servings:** 8 **Yield:** 16 macarons

Ingredients

- 3 large egg whites egg whites
- ¼ cup white sugar
- 1 ⅔ cups confectioners' sugar
- 1 cup finely ground almonds

Directions

Step 1

Line a baking sheet with a silicone baking mat.

Step 2

Beat egg whites in the bowl of a stand mixer fitted with a whisk attachment until whites are foamy; beat in white sugar and continue beating until egg whites are glossy, fluffy, and hold soft peaks. Sift confectioners' sugar and ground almonds in a separate bowl and quickly fold the almond mixture into the egg whites, about 30 strokes.

Step 3

Spoon a small amount of batter into a plastic bag with a small corner cut off and pipe a test disk of batter, about 1 1/2 inches in diameter, onto prepared baking sheet. If the disk of batter holds a peak instead of flattening immediately, gently fold the batter a few more times and retest.

Step 4

When batter is mixed enough to flatten immediately into an even disk, spoon into a pastry bag fitted with a plain round tip. Pipe the batter onto the baking sheet in rounds, leaving space between the disks. Let the piped cookies stand out at room temperature until they form a hard skin on top, about 1 hour.

Step 5

Preheat oven to 285 degrees F (140 degrees C).

Step 6

Bake cookies until set but not browned, about 10 minutes; let cookies cool completely before filling.

Nutrition Facts

Per Serving:

189.5 calories; protein 6.9g 14% DV; carbohydrates 36.4g 12% DV; fat 2.6g 4% DV; cholesterolmg; sodium 22mg 1% DV.

Peanut Butter Bars I

Prep: 25 mins **Additional:** 1 hr **Total:** 1 hr 25 mins **Servings:** 12 **Yield:** 1 - 9x13 inch pan

Ingredients

- 1 cup butter or margarine, melted
- 2 cups graham cracker crumbs
- 2 cups confectioners' sugar
- 1 cup peanut butter
- 1 ½ cups semisweet chocolate chips
- 4 tablespoons peanut butter

Directions

Step 1

In a medium bowl, mix together the butter or margarine, graham cracker crumbs, confectioners' sugar, and 1 cup peanut butter until well blended. Press evenly into the bottom of an ungreased 9x13 inch pan.

Step 2

In a metal bowl over simmering water, or in the microwave, melt the chocolate chips with the 4 tablespoons peanut butter, stirring occasionally until smooth. Spread over the prepared crust. Refrigerate for at least one hour before cutting into squares.

Nutrition Facts

Per Serving:

531.5 calories; protein 8.8g 18% DV; carbohydrates 49.2g 16% DV; fat 36.6g 56% DV; cholesterol 40.7mg 14% DV; sodium 319.7mg 13% DV.

Biscotti

Prep: 15 mins **Cook:** 25 mins **Total:** 40 mins **Servings:** 42 **Yield:** 3 to 4 dozen

Ingredients

- ½ cup vegetable oil
- 1 cup white sugar
- 3 ¼ cups all-purpose flour
- 3 large eggs eggs
- 1 tablespoon baking powder
- 1 tablespoon anise extract, or 3 drops anise oil

Directions

Step 1

Preheat the oven to 375 degrees F (190 degrees C). Grease cookie sheets or line with parchment paper.

Step 2

In a medium bowl, beat together the oil, eggs, sugar and anise flavoring until well blended. Combine the flour and baking powder, stir into the egg mixture to form a heavy dough. Divide dough into two pieces. Form each piece into a roll as long as your cookie sheet. Place roll onto the prepared cookie sheet, and press down to 1/2 inch thickness.

Step 3

Bake for 25 to 30 minutes in the preheated oven, until golden brown. Remove from the baking sheet to cool on a wire rack. When The cookies are cool enough to handle, slice each one crosswise into 1/2 inch slices. Place the slices cut side up back onto the baking sheet. Bake for an additional 6 to 10 minutes on each side. Slices should be lightly toasted.

Nutrition Facts

Per Serving:

82.8 calories; protein 1.4g 3% DV; carbohydrates 12.3g 4% DV; fat 3.1g 5% DV; cholesterol 13.3mg 4% DV; sodium 40mg 2% DV.

Award Winning Soft Chocolate Chip Cookies

Prep: 15 mins **Cook:** 12 mins **Additional:** 1 hr 13 mins **Total:** 1 hr 40 mins **Servings:** 72 **Yield:** 6 dozen

Ingredients

- 4 ½ cups all-purpose flour
- 2 teaspoons baking soda
- 2 cups butter, softened
- 1 ½ cups packed brown sugar
- ½ cup white sugar
- 2 (3.4 ounce) packages instant vanilla pudding mix
- 4 large eggs eggs
- 2 teaspoons vanilla extract
- 4 cups semisweet chocolate chips
- 2 cups chopped walnuts

Directions

Step 1

Preheat oven to 350 degrees F (175 degrees C). Sift together the flour and baking soda, set aside.

Step 2

In a large bowl, cream together the butter, brown sugar, and white sugar. Beat in the instant pudding mix until blended. Stir in the eggs and vanilla. Blend in the flour mixture. Finally, stir in the chocolate chips and nuts. Drop cookies by rounded spoonfuls onto ungreased cookie sheets.

Step 3

Bake for 10 to 12 minutes in the preheated oven. Edges should be golden brown.

Nutrition Facts

Per Serving:

177 calories; protein 2.1g 4% DV; carbohydrates 20.7g 7% DV; fat 10.5g 16% DV; cholesterol 23.9mg 8% DV; sodium 115.8mg 5% DV.

Brooke's Best Bombshell Brownies

Prep: 15 mins **Cook:** 35 mins **Total:** 50 mins **Servings:** 24 **Yield:** 24 servings

Ingredients

- 1 cup butter, melted
- 3 cups white sugar
- 1 tablespoon vanilla extract
- 4 large eggs eggs

- 1 ½ cups all-purpose flour
- 1 cup unsweetened cocoa powder
- 1 teaspoon salt
- 1 cup semisweet chocolate chips

Directions

Step 1

Preheat oven to 350 degrees F (175 degrees C). Lightly grease a 9x13 baking dish.

Step 2

Combine the melted butter, sugar, and vanilla in a large bowl. Beat in the eggs, one at a time, mixing well after each, until thoroughly blended.

Step 3

Sift the flour, cocoa powder, and salt in a bowl. Gradually stir flour mixture into the egg mixture until blended. Stir in the chocolate morsels. Spread the batter evenly into the prepared baking dish.

Step 4

Bake in preheated oven until an inserted toothpick comes out clean, 35 to 40 minutes. Remove, and cool pan on wire rack before cutting.

Per Serving:

248.2 calories; protein 2.9g 6% DV; carbohydrates 37.5g 12% DV; fat 11.2g 17% DV; cholesterol 51.3mg 17% DV; sodium 164.8mg 7% DV.

Coconut Macaroons III

Prep: 10 mins **Additional:** 15 mins **Total:** 25 mins **Servings:** 12 **Yield:** 1 dozen

Ingredients

- ⅔ cup all-purpose flour
- 5 ½ cups flaked coconut
- ¼ teaspoon salt

- 1 (14 ounce) can sweetened condensed milk
- 2 teaspoons vanilla extract

Directions

Step 1

Preheat oven to 350 degrees F (175 degrees C). Line cookie sheets with parchment paper or aluminum foil.

Step 2

In a large bowl, stir together the flour, coconut and salt. Stir in the sweetened condensed milk and vanilla using your hands until well blended. Use an ice cream scoop to drop dough onto the prepared cookie sheets. Cookies should be about golf ball size.

Step 3

Bake for 12 to 15 minutes in the preheated oven, until coconut is toasted.

Nutrition Facts

Per Serving:

286.9 calories; protein 4.4g 9% DV; carbohydrates 40.7g 13% DV; fat 12.4g 19% DV; cholesterol 11.1mg 4% DV; sodium 186.8mg 8% DV.

Nanaimo Bars III

Prep: 30 mins **Total:** 30 mins **Servings:** 16 **Yield:** 1 8x8-inch pan

Ingredients

- ½ cup butter, softened
- ¼ cup white sugar
- 5 tablespoons unsweetened cocoa powder
- 1 egg, beaten
- 1 ¾ cups graham cracker crumbs
- 1 cup flaked coconut
- ½ cup finely chopped almonds

- ½ cup butter, softened
- 3 tablespoons heavy cream
- 2 tablespoons custard powder
- 2 cups confectioners' sugar
- 4 (1 ounce) squares semisweet baking chocolate
- 2 teaspoons butter

Directions

Step 1

In the top of a double boiler, combine 1/2 cup butter, white sugar and cocoa powder. Stir occasionally until melted and smooth. Beat in the egg, stirring until thick, 2 to 3 minutes. Remove from heat and mix in the graham cracker crumbs, coconut and almonds (if you like). Press into the bottom of an ungreased 8x8 inch pan.

Step 2

For the middle layer, cream together 1/2 cup butter, heavy cream and custard powder until light and fluffy. Mix in the confectioners' sugar until smooth. Spread over the bottom layer in the pan. Chill to set.

Step 3

While the second layer is chilling, melt the semisweet chocolate and 2 teaspoons butter together in the microwave or over low heat. Spread over the chilled bars. Let the chocolate set before cutting into squares.

Nutrition Facts

Per Serving:

310.5 calories; protein 2.8g 6% DV; carbohydrates 34.1g 11% DV; fat 19.6g 30% DV; cholesterol 47.3mg 16% DV; sodium 160.1mg 6% DV.

Peanut Butter Cup Cookies

Prep: 25 mins **Cook:** 10 mins **Additional:** 1 hr **Total:** 1 hr 35 mins **Servings:** 40 **Yield:** 40 cookies

Ingredients

- 1 ¾ cups all-purpose flour
- ½ teaspoon salt
- 1 teaspoon baking soda
- ½ cup butter, softened

- ½ cup white sugar
- ½ cup peanut butter
- ½ cup packed brown sugar
- 1 egg, beaten

- 1 teaspoon vanilla extract
- 2 tablespoons milk
- 40 eaches miniature chocolate covered peanut butter cups, unwrapped

Directions

Step 1

Preheat oven to 375 degrees F (190 degrees C). Sift together the flour, salt and baking soda; set aside.

Step 2

Cream together the butter, sugar, peanut butter and brown sugar until fluffy. Beat in the egg, vanilla and milk. Add the flour mixture; mix well. Shape into 40 balls and place each into an ungreased mini muffin pan.

Step 3

Bake at 375 degrees for about 8 minutes. Remove from oven and immediately press a mini peanut butter cup into each ball. Cool and carefully remove from pan.

Nutrition Facts

Per Serving:

122 calories; protein 2.4g 5% DV; carbohydrates 14.4g 5% DV; fat 6.5g 10% DV; cholesterol 11.3mg 4% DV; sodium 119.1mg 5% DV.

Scotcharoos

Prep: 15 mins **Cook:** 15 mins **Additional:** 1 hr **Total:** 1 hr 30 mins **Servings:** 24 **Yield:** 24 bars

Ingredients

- 1 cup light corn syrup
- 1 cup white sugar
- 1 ½ cups peanut butter
- 6 cups crisp rice cereal
- ½ cup semisweet chocolate chips
- ½ cup butterscotch chips

Directions

Step 1

Generously butter a 9x13 inch baking pan. Set aside.

Step 2

In a large pot, mix together corn syrup, sugar, and peanut butter. Cook over medium heat, stirring until peanut butter melts. Bring mixture to a boil. Remove from heat, and stir in crisp rice cereal.

Step 3

Transfer mixture into a well buttered 9x13 inch pan. With your hands well buttered, pat it down into pan.

Step 4

In a medium saucepan, over medium low heat, melt chocolate chips and butterscotch chips until smooth. Spread over top of bars and let bars cool. Cut into squares.

Nutrition Facts

Per Serving:

239.8 calories; protein 4.9g 10% DV; carbohydrates 33.8g 11% DV; fat 10.6g 16% DV; cholesterolmg; sodium 139.7mg 6% DV.

Molasses Cookies

Prep: 10 mins **Cook:** 10 mins **Additional:** 1 hr **Total:** 1 hr 20 mins **Servings:** 30 **Yield:** 5 dozen

Ingredients

- ¾ cup margarine, melted
- 1 cup white sugar
- 1 egg
- ¼ cup molasses
- 2 cups all-purpose flour
- 2 teaspoons baking soda
- ½ teaspoon salt
- 1 teaspoon ground cinnamon
- ½ teaspoon ground cloves
- ½ teaspoon ground ginger
- ½ cup white sugar

Directions

Step 1

In a medium bowl, mix together the melted margarine, 1 cup sugar, and egg until smooth. Stir in the molasses. Combine the flour, baking soda, salt, cinnamon, cloves, and ginger; blend into the molasses mixture. Cover, and chill dough for 1 hour.

Step 2

Preheat oven to 375 degrees F (190 degrees C). Roll dough into walnut sized balls, and roll them in the remaining white sugar. Place cookies 2 inches apart onto ungreased baking sheets.

Step 3

Bake for 8 to 10 minutes in the preheated oven, until tops are cracked. Cool on wire racks.

Nutrition Facts

Per Serving:

119.8 calories; protein 1.1g 2% DV; carbohydrates 18.6g 6% DV; fat 4.7g 7% DV; cholesterol 6.2mg 2% DV; sodium 178.8mg 7% DV.

Easy Lemon Cookies

Servings: 36 **Yield:** 3 dozen cookies

Ingredients

- 1 (18.25 ounce) package lemon cake mix
- 2 large eggs eggs
- ⅓ cup vegetable oil
- 1 teaspoon lemon extract
- ⅓ cup confectioners' sugar for decoration

Directions

Step 1

Preheat oven to 375 degrees F (190 degrees C).

Step 2

Pour cake mix into a large bowl. Stir in eggs, oil, and lemon extract until well blended. Drop teaspoonfuls of dough into a bowl of confectioners' sugar. Roll them around until they're lightly covered. Once sugared, put them on an ungreased cookie sheet.

Step 3

Bake for 6 to 9 minutes in the preheated oven. The bottoms will be light brown, and the insides chewy.

Nutrition Facts

Per Serving:

87.1 calories; protein 1.2g 2% DV; carbohydrates 11.6g 4% DV; fat 4g 6% DV; cholesterol 14mg 5% DV; sodium 106.7mg 4% DV.

Gramma's Date Squares

Prep: 25 mins **Cook:** 25 mins **Total:** 50 mins **Servings:** 12 **Yield:** 1 -9x9 inch pan

Ingredients

- 1 ½ cups rolled oats
- 1 ½ cups sifted pastry flour
- ¼ teaspoon salt
- ¾ teaspoon baking soda
- 1 cup packed brown sugar
- ¾ cup butter, softened
- ¾ pound pitted dates, diced
- 1 cup water
- ⅓ cup packed brown sugar
- 1 teaspoon lemon juice

Directions

Step 1

Preheat oven to 350 degrees F (175 degrees C).

Step 2

In a large bowl, combine oats, pastry flour, salt, 1 cup brown sugar, and baking soda. Mix in the butter until crumbly. Press half of the mixture into the bottom of a 9 inch square baking pan.

Step 3

In a small saucepan over medium heat, combine the dates, water, and 1/3 cup brown sugar. Bring to a boil, and cook until thickened. Stir in lemon juice, and remove from heat. Spread the filling over the base, and pat the remaining crumb mixture on top.

Step 4

Bake for 20 to 25 minutes in preheated oven, or until top is lightly toasted. Cool before cutting into squares.

Nutrition Facts

Per Serving:

363.1 calories; protein 3.7g 7% DV; carbohydrates 63.7g 21% DV; fat 12.5g 19% DV; cholesterol 30.5mg 10% DV; sodium 217.4mg 9% DV.

Thumbprint Cookies I

Servings: 12 **Yield:** 2 dozen

Ingredients

- ½ cup butter, softened
- ¼ cup packed brown sugar
- 1 egg
- ½ teaspoon vanilla extract
- 1 cup all-purpose flour
- ¼ cup finely chopped walnuts
- ⅔ cup any flavor fruit jam
- ¼ teaspoon salt

Directions

Step 1

Preheat oven to 300 degrees F. Grease cookie sheets.

Step 2

Separate egg, reserving egg white. Cream butter or margarine, sugar, and egg yolk.

Step 3

Add vanilla, flour and salt, mixing well.

Step 4

Shape dough into balls. Roll in egg white, then walnuts. Place on cookie sheets about 2 inches apart. Bake for 5 minutes.

Step 5

Remove cookies from oven. With thumb, dent each cookie. Put jelly or preserves in each thumbprint. Bake for another 8 minutes.

Nutrition Facts

Per Serving:

194.6 calories; protein 2.1g 4% DV; carbohydrates 25g 8% DV; fat 9.8g 15% DV; cholesterol 35.8mg 12% DV; sodium 116mg 5% DV.

Cranberry Orange Cookies

Prep: 20 mins **Cook:** 14 mins **Total:** 34 mins **Servings:** 48 **Yield:** 4 dozen cookies

Ingredients

- 1 cup butter, softened
- 1 cup white sugar
- ½ cup packed brown sugar
- 1 egg
- 1 teaspoon grated orange zest
- 2 tablespoons orange juice
- 2 ½ cups all-purpose flour
- ½ teaspoon baking soda
- ½ teaspoon salt
- 2 cups chopped cranberries
- ½ cup chopped walnuts
- ½ teaspoon grated orange zest
- 3 tablespoons orange juice
- 1 ½ cups confectioners' sugar

Directions

Step 1

Preheat the oven to 375 degrees F (190 degrees C).

Step 2

In a large bowl, cream together the butter, white sugar and brown sugar until smooth. Beat in the egg until well blended. Mix in 1 teaspoon orange zest and 2 tablespoons orange juice. Combine the flour, baking soda and salt; stir into the orange mixture. Mix in cranberries and if using, walnuts, until evenly distributed. Drop dough by rounded tablespoonfuls onto ungreased cookie sheets. Cookies should be spaced at least 2 inches apart.

Step 3

Bake for 12 to 14 minutes in the preheated oven, until the edges are golden. Remove from cookie sheets to cool on wire racks.

Step 4

In a small bowl, mix together 1/2 teaspoon orange zest, 3 tablespoons orange juice and confectioners' sugar until smooth. Spread over the tops of cooled cookies. Let stand until set.

Nutrition Facts

Per Serving:

110.2 calories; protein 1.1g 2% DV; carbohydrates 16.2g 5% DV; fat 4.8g 7% DV; cholesterol 14mg 5% DV; sodium 67mg 3% DV.

Caramel Shortbread Squares

Prep: 10 mins **Cook:** 25 mins **Total:** 35 mins **Servings:** 40 **Yield:** 1 - 9x9 inch pan

Ingredients

- ⅔ cup butter, softened
- ¼ cup white sugar
- 1 ¼ cups all-purpose flour
- ½ cup butter

- ½ cup packed light brown sugar
- 2 tablespoons light corn syrup
- ½ cup sweetened condensed milk
- 1 ¼ cups milk chocolate chips

Directions

Step 1

Preheat oven to 350 degrees F (175 C).

Step 2

In a medium bowl, mix together 2/3 cup butter, white sugar, and flour until evenly crumbly. Press into a 9 inch square baking pan. Bake for 20 minutes.

Step 3

In a 2 quart saucepan, combine 1/2 cup butter, brown sugar, corn syrup, and sweetened condensed milk. Bring to a boil. Continue to boil for 5 minutes. Remove from heat and beat vigorously with a wooden spoon for about 3 minutes. Pour over baked crust (warm or cool). Cool until it begins to firm.

Step 4

Place chocolate in a microwave-safe bowl. Heat for 1 minute, then stir and continue to heat and stir at 20 second intervals until chocolate is melted and smooth. Pour chocolate over the caramel layer and spread evenly to cover completely. Chill. Cut into 1 inch squares. These need to be small because they are so rich.

Nutrition Facts

Per Serving:

118.7 calories; protein 1.1g 2% DV; carbohydrates 13.2g 4% DV; fat 7.3g 11% DV; cholesterol 16.7mg 6% DV; sodium 44.5mg 2% DV.

White Chocolate and Cranberry Cookies

Prep: 15 mins **Cook:** 10 mins **Additional:** 25 mins **Total:** 50 mins **Servings:** 24 **Yield:** 2 dozen

Ingredients

- ½ cup butter, softened
- ½ cup packed brown sugar
- ½ cup white sugar
- 1 egg
- 1 tablespoon brandy
- 1 ½ cups all-purpose flour
- ½ teaspoon baking soda
- ¾ cup white chocolate chips
- 1 cup dried cranberries

Directions

Step 1

Preheat oven to 375 degrees F (190 degrees C). Grease cookie sheets.

Step 2

In a large bowl, cream together the butter, brown sugar, and white sugar until smooth. Beat in the egg and brandy. Combine the flour and baking soda; stir into the sugar mixture. Mix in the white chocolate chips and cranberries. Drop by heaping spoonfuls onto prepared cookie sheets.

Step 3

Bake for 8 to 10 minutes in the preheated oven. For best results, take them out while they are still doughy. Allow cookies to cool for 1 minute on the cookie sheets before transferring to wire racks to cool completely.

Nutrition Facts

Per Serving:

147.4 calories; protein 1.5g 3% DV; carbohydrates 21.9g 7% DV; fat 6.1g 9% DV; cholesterol 19.1mg 6% DV; sodium 63.8mg 3% DV.

Buckeye Balls II

Prep: 45 mins **Cook:** 10 mins **Additional:** 30 mins **Total:** 1 hr 25 mins **Servings:** 30 **Yield:** 5 dozen

Ingredients

- 1 ½ cups creamy peanut butter
- ½ cup butter, softened
- 1 teaspoon vanilla extract
- 4 cups sifted confectioners' sugar
- 6 ounces semi-sweet chocolate chips
- 2 tablespoons shortening

Directions

Step 1

Line a baking sheet with waxed paper; set aside.

Step 2

In a medium bowl, mix peanut butter, butter, vanilla, and confectioners' sugar with hands to form a smooth stiff dough. Shape into balls using 2 teaspoons of dough for each ball. Place on prepared pan, and refrigerate.

Step 3

Melt shortening and chocolate together in a metal bowl over a pan of lightly simmering water. Stir occasionally until smooth, and remove from heat.

Step 4

Remove balls from refrigerator. Insert a wooden toothpick into a ball, and dip into melted chocolate. Return to wax paper, chocolate side down, and remove toothpick. Repeat with remaining balls. Refrigerate for 30 minutes to set.

Nutrition Facts

203.6 calories; protein 3.7g 7% DV; carbohydrates 22.8g 7% DV; fat 12g 19% DV; cholesterol 8.1mg 3% DV; sodium 81.2mg 3% DV.

Fresh Ginger Cookies

Prep: 30 mins **Cook:** 15 mins **Additional:** 1 hr **Total:** 1 hr 45 mins **Servings:** 30 **Yield:** 30 cookies

Ingredients

- 2 ¼ cups all-purpose flour
- 1 teaspoon baking soda
- ½ teaspoon salt
- 2 tablespoons grated fresh ginger
- ¾ cup butter, softened
- 1 cup white sugar
- ¼ cup molasses
- 1 egg
- 1 cup white sugar

Directions

Step 1

In a large mixing bowl, combine flour, soda, and salt. In a separate bowl, beat ginger, butter, and 1 cup sugar until light and fluffy. Beat in molasses and egg. Gently fold in flour mixture until just combined. Chill for 1 hour.

Step 2

Preheat oven to 350 degrees F (175 degrees C).

Step 3

Roll dough into 1 1/2 inch balls and then roll them in sugar. Place 2 inches apart on ungreased baking sheets.

Step 4

Bake until edges start to brown, about 15 minutes. Centers will be slightly soft. Let stand on cookie sheets 1 minute and remove to racks to cool completely.

Nutrition Facts

Per Serving:

137 calories; protein 1.2g 3% DV; carbohydrates 22.6g 7% DV; fat 4.9g 8% DV; cholesterol 18.4mg 6% DV; sodium 117mg 5% DV.

Oatmeal Chocolate Coconut Macaroons

Prep: 15 mins **Cook:** 5 mins **Total:** 20 mins **Servings:** 15 **Yield:** 15 cookies

Ingredients

- 2 cups quick-cooking oats
- 1 cup shredded coconut
- ¼ cup unsweetened cocoa powder
- 2 cups white sugar
- ½ cup butter
- ½ cup milk

Directions

Step 1

Mix oats, coconut, and cocoa powder together in a bowl.

Step 2

Bring sugar, butter, and milk to a boil in saucepan, stirring occasionally; remove immediately from heat and stir into oat mixture.

Step 3

Drop 15 spoonfuls of batter onto a sheet of waxed paper. Cool to room temperature before serving.

Nutrition Facts

Per Serving:

228.2 calories; protein 2.2g 4% DV; carbohydrates 37.7g 12% DV; fat 8.6g 13% DV; cholesterol 16.9mg 6% DV; sodium 61.9mg 3% DV.

Cracked Sugar Cookies I

Servings: 24 **Yield:** 4 dozen

Ingredients

- 1 ¼ cups white sugar
- 1 cup butter
- 3 large egg yolks egg yolks
- 1 teaspoon vanilla extract

- 2 ½ cups all-purpose flour
- 1 teaspoon baking soda
- ½ teaspoon cream of tartar

Directions

Step 1

Preheat oven to 350 degrees F (180 degrees C). Lightly grease 2 cookie sheets.

Step 2

Cream together sugar and butter. Beat in egg yolks and vanilla.

Step 3

Add flour, baking soda, and cream of tartar. Stir.

Step 4

Form dough into walnut size balls and place 2 inches apart on cookie sheet. Don't flatten. Bake 10 to 11 minutes, until tops are cracked and just turning color.

Nutrition Facts

Per Serving:

162.8 calories; protein 1.8g 4% DV; carbohydrates 20.5g 7% DV; fat 8.4g 13% DV; cholesterol 45.9mg 15% DV; sodium 108.2mg 4% DV.

Cowboy Cookie Mix in a Jar

Prep: 25 mins **Total:** 25 mins **Servings:** 18 **Yield:** 3 dozen cookies

Ingredients

- 1 ⅓ cups rolled oats
- ½ cup packed brown sugar
- ½ cup white sugar
- ½ cup chopped pecans

- 1 cup semisweet chocolate chips
- 1 ⅓ cups all-purpose flour
- 1 teaspoon baking powder
- 1 teaspoon baking soda

- ¼ teaspoon salt

Directions

Step 1

Layer the ingredients in a 1 quart jar in the order given. Press each layer firmly in place before adding the next layer.

Step 2

Include a card with the following instructions: Cowboy Cookie Mix in a Jar 1. Preheat oven to 350 degrees F (175 degrees C). Grease cookie sheets. 2. In a medium bowl, mix together 1/2 cup melted butter or margarine, 1 egg, and 1 teaspoon of vanilla. Stir in the entire contents of the jar. You may need to use your hands to finish mixing. Shape into walnut sized balls. Place 2 inches apart on prepared cookie sheets. 3. Bake for 11 to 13 minutes in the preheated oven. Transfer from cookie sheets to cool on wire racks.

Nutrition Facts

Per Serving:

166.9 calories; protein 2.4g 5% DV; carbohydrates 29.1g 9% DV; fat 5.5g 8% DV; cholesterolmg; sodium 132.6mg 5% DV.

Rosettes I

Prep: 15 mins **Cook:** 1 hr 30 mins **Total:** 1 hr 45 mins **Servings:** 30 **Yield:** 5 dozen

Ingredients

- 2 large eggs eggs
- 1 tablespoon white sugar
- 1 cup sifted all-purpose flour
- 1 cup milk
- 1 teaspoon vanilla extract
- ¼ teaspoon salt
- vegetable oil for frying
- sifted confectioners' sugar

Directions

Step 1

Combine eggs, sugar and salt; beat well. Add remaining ingredients and beat until smooth.

Step 2

Heat a rosette iron in deep, hot oil (375 degrees) for 2 minutes.

Step 3

Drain excess oil from iron. Dip in batter to 1/4 inch from the top of the iron, then dip iron immediately into hot oil (375 degrees).

Step 4

Fry rosette until golden, about 30 seconds. Lift out; tip upside down to drain. With fork, push rosette off iron onto a rack placed over paper towels.

Step 5

Reheat iron 1 minute; make next rosette.

Step 6

Sprinkle rosettes with confectioners' sugar.

Nutrition Facts

Per Serving:

560.9 calories; protein 1.1g 2% DV; carbohydrates 8.2g 3% DV; fat 59.2g 91% DV; cholesterol 13.1mg 4% DV; sodium 27.5mg 1% DV.

Whipped Shortbread Cookies

Prep: 15 mins **Cook:** 20 mins **Total:** 35 mins **Servings:** 36 **Yield:** 3 dozen

Ingredients

- 1 cup butter, softened
- 1 ½ cups all-purpose flour
- ½ cup confectioners' sugar
- ¼ cup red maraschino cherries, quartered
- ¼ cup green maraschino cherries, quartered

Directions

Step 1

Preheat oven to 350 degrees F (175 degrees C).

Step 2

In a large bowl, combine butter, flour, and confectioners' sugar. With an electric mixer, beat for 10 minutes, until light and fluffy. Spoon onto cookie sheets, spacing cookies 2 inches apart. Place a piece of maraschino cherry onto the middle of each cookie, alternating between red and green.

Step 3

Bake for 15 to 17 minutes in the preheated oven, or until the bottoms of the cookies are lightly browned. Remove from oven, and let cool on cookie sheet for 5 minutes, then transfer cookies on to wire rack to cool. Store in an airtight container, separating each layer with waxed paper.

Nutrition Facts

Per Serving:

74.8 calories; protein 0.6g 1% DV; carbohydrates 6.8g 2% DV; fat 5.2g 8% DV; cholesterol 13.6mg 5% DV; sodium 36.5mg 2% DV.

Molasses Crinkles

Servings: 48 **Yield:** 3 -4 dozen

Ingredients

- ¾ cup shortening
- 1 cup packed brown sugar
- 1 egg
- ¼ cup molasses
- 2 ¼ cups all-purpose flour
- 2 teaspoons baking soda
- ¼ teaspoon salt
- ½ teaspoon ground cloves
- 1 teaspoon ground cinnamon
- 1 teaspoon ground ginger
- ⅓ cup granulated sugar for decoration

Directions

Step 1

Cream the shortening and the brown sugar. Stir in the egg and molasses and mix well.

Step 2

Combine the flour, baking soda, salt, cloves, cinnamon, and ginger. Add the flour mixture to the shortening mixture and mix well. Cover and chill dough for at least 2 to 3 hours.

Step 3

Preheat oven to 350 degrees F (175 degrees C). Grease cookie sheets.

Step 4

Roll dough into balls the size of large walnuts. Roll balls in sugar and place 3 inches apart on the prepared baking sheets. Bake at 350 degrees F (175 degrees C) for 10 to 12 minutes. Let cool for one minute before transferring to a wire rack to continue cooling.

Nutrition Facts

Per Serving:

79.2 calories; protein 0.7g 2% DV; carbohydrates 11.7g 4% DV; fat 3.4g 5% DV; cholesterol 3.9mg 1% DV; sodium 68.1mg 3% DV.

Sugar Cookies with Buttercream Frosting

Prep: 15 mins **Cook:** 5 mins **Additional:** 2 hrs **Total:** 2 hrs 20 mins **Servings:** 60 **Yield:** 5 dozen

Ingredients

- 1 cup butter
- 1 cup white sugar
- 2 large eggs eggs
- ½ teaspoon vanilla extract
- 3 ¼ cups all-purpose flour
- ½ teaspoon baking powder
- ½ teaspoon baking soda

- ½ teaspoon salt
- ½ cup shortening
- 1 pound confectioners' sugar
- 5 tablespoons water
- ¼ teaspoon salt
- ½ teaspoon vanilla extract
- ¼ teaspoon butter flavored extract

Directions

Step 1

In a large bowl, mix together butter, sugar, eggs, and vanilla with an electric mixer until light and fluffy. Combine the flour, baking powder, baking soda, and salt; gradually stir flour mixture into butter mixture until well blended using a sturdy spoon. Chill dough for 2 hours.

Step 2

Preheat the oven to 400 degrees F (200 degrees C). On a lightly floured surface, roll out the dough to 1/4 inch thickness. Cut into desired shapes using cookie cutters. Place cookies 2 inches apart onto ungreased cookie sheets.

Step 3

Bake for 4 to 6 minutes in the preheated oven. Remove cookies from pan and cool on wire racks.

Step 4

Using an electric mixer, beat shortening, confectioners sugar, water, salt, vanilla extract, and butter flavoring until fluffy. Frost cookies after they have cooled completely.

Nutrition Facts

Per Serving:

111.8 calories; protein 0.9g 2% DV; carbohydrates 16.1g 5% DV; fat 5g 8% DV; cholesterol 14.3mg 5% DV; sodium 68mg 3% DV.

Butterscotch Drops

Prep: 10 mins **Cook:** 5 mins **Additional:** 1 hr **Total:** 1 hr 15 mins **Servings:** 24 **Yield:** 24 cookies

Ingredients

- 1 (11 ounce) package butterscotch chips
- 1 cup creamy peanut butter
- 4 cups cornflakes cereal

Directions

Step 1

In a medium saucepan over medium heat, melt butterscotch chips and peanut butter together. Remove from stove and stir in cornflakes. Drop by spoonfuls onto cookie sheets. Chill to harden.

Nutrition Facts

Per Serving:

152.5 calories; protein 3g 6% DV; carbohydrates 14.3g 5% DV; fat 9.1g 14% DV; cholesterolmg; sodium 96.7mg 4% DV.

Gingerbread Biscotti

Prep: 25 mins **Cook:** 40 mins **Total:** 1 hr 5 mins **Servings:** 48 **Yield:** 4 dozen

Ingredients

- ⅓ cup vegetable oil
- 1 cup white sugar
- 3 large eggs eggs
- ¼ cup molasses
- 2 ¼ cups all-purpose flour
- 1 cup whole wheat flour

- 1 tablespoon baking powder
- 1 ½ tablespoons ground ginger
- ¾ tablespoon ground cinnamon
- ½ tablespoon ground cloves
- ¼ teaspoon ground nutmeg

Directions

Step 1

Preheat the oven to 375 degrees F (190 degrees C). Grease a cookie sheet.

Step 2

In a large bowl, mix together oil, sugar, eggs, and molasses. In another bowl, combine flours, baking powder, ginger, cinnamon, cloves, and nutmeg; mix into egg mixture to form a stiff dough.

Step 3

Divide dough in half, and shape each half into a roll the length of the cookie. Place rolls on cookie sheet, and pat down to flatten the dough to 1/2 inch thickness.

Step 4

Bake in preheated oven for 25 minutes. Remove from oven, and set aside to cool.

Step 5

When cool enough to touch, cut into 1/2 inch thick diagonal slices. Place sliced biscotti on cookie sheet, and bake an additional 5 to 7 minutes on each side, or until toasted and crispy.

Nutrition Facts

Per Serving:

70 calories; protein 1.4g 3% DV; carbohydrates 12.1g 4% DV; fat 2g 3% DV; cholesterol 11.6mg 4% DV; sodium 26.5mg 1% DV.

Rosenmunnar

Prep: 40 mins **Cook:** 15 mins **Total:** 55 mins **Servings:** 36 **Yield:** 3 dozen

Ingredients

- 1 cup butter, softened
- ½ cup white sugar
- 2 cups sifted all-purpose flour
- ½ cup any flavor fruit jam

Directions

Step 1

Preheat oven to 375 degrees F (190 degrees C).

Step 2

Cream butter and sugar until light and fluffy. Add sifted flour, and mix well. Shape dough into 1-inch balls and place on cookie sheets. Imprint your thumb in the center to make a 1/2-inch indentation. Fill with your favorite preserves.

Step 3

Bake 15 to 20 minutes or until golden brown at the edges.

Nutrition Facts

Per Serving:

93.5 calories; protein 0.8g 2% DV; carbohydrates 11.1g 4% DV; fat 5.2g 8% DV; cholesterol 13.6mg 5% DV; sodium 37.9mg 2% DV.

Meatball Cookies

Servings: 30 **Yield:** 5 dozen

Ingredients

- 3 cups all-purpose flour
- ⅔ cup unsweetened cocoa powder
- 1 ½ teaspoons baking powder
- 1 ½ teaspoons baking soda
- 1 teaspoon salt
- 1 cup chopped walnuts
- 1 teaspoon ground cloves
- 1 teaspoon ground allspice
- 1 teaspoon ground cinnamon
- ½ teaspoon ground nutmeg
- 1 ½ cups white sugar
- 3 large eggs eggs
- ½ cup butter
- 2 teaspoons vanilla extract
- 4 cups confectioners' sugar
- ¼ cup unsweetened cocoa powder
- ½ cup milk

Directions

Step 1

Preheat oven to 350 degrees F (180 degrees C). Grease cookie sheets.

Step 2

Cream the butter margarine or shortening, white sugar, eggs and vanilla.

Step 3

In a separate bowl, stir the flour, 2/3 cup cocoa, baking powder, baking soda, salt and spices. Add flour mixture to butter mixture. If too sticky add more flour, if too dry add a little milk. Add nuts and mix with hands. Must be of consistency to roll into little 1/2 - 1 inch balls.

Step 4

After you have cookie dough to handling consistency by adjusting it with either the flour or milk, roll into little balls, place on the cookie sheet and bake for about 10-12 minutes, cookie should be firm. Do not overcook. Remove from oven, let rest on the sheet for a few moments and remove to wax paper. When cool, frost with confectioner's sugar and cocoa glaze.

Step 5

To Make Glaze: Combine 4 cups confectioner's sugar, 1/4 cup cocoa, add about 1/2 cup milk. Consistency should be of a glaze. Pour small amount of glaze over each cookie (about 1 tsp.). Decorate with sprinkles while glaze is still wet.

Nutrition Facts

Per Serving:

216.1 calories; protein 3.2g 6% DV; carbohydrates 37.9g 12% DV; fat 6.7g 10% DV; cholesterol 27.1mg 9% DV; sodium 196.6mg 8% DV.

Gingerbread Men

Prep: 25 mins **Cook:** 12 mins **Additional:** 1 hr **Total:** 1 hr 37 mins **Servings:** 30 **Yield:** 2 1/2 dozen

Ingredients

- 1 (3.5 ounce) package cook and serve butterscotch pudding mix
- ½ cup butter
- ½ cup packed brown sugar
- 1 egg

- 1 ½ cups all-purpose flour
- ½ teaspoon baking soda
- 1 ½ teaspoons ground ginger
- 1 teaspoon ground cinnamon

Directions

Step 1

In a medium bowl, cream together the dry butterscotch pudding mix, butter, and brown sugar until smooth. Stir in the egg. Combine the flour, baking soda, ginger, and cinnamon; stir into the pudding mixture. Cover, and chill dough until firm, about 1 hour.

Step 2

Preheat the oven to 350 degrees F (175 degrees C). Grease baking sheets. On a floured board, roll dough out to about 1/8 inch thickness, and cut into man shapes using a cookie cutter. Place cookies 2 inches apart on the prepared baking sheets.

Step 3

Bake for 10 to 12 minutes in the preheated oven, until cookies are golden at the edges. Cool on wire racks.

Nutrition Facts

Per Serving:

79.3 calories; protein 1g 2% DV; carbohydrates 11.5g 4% DV; fat 3.3g 5% DV; cholesterol 14.3mg 5% DV; sodium 62.6mg 3% DV.

Peanut Butter Balls IV

Servings: 30 **Yield:** 5 dozen

Ingredients

- ¼ cup butter
- 1 ½ cups peanut butter
- 4 cups confectioners' sugar
- 1 teaspoon vanilla extract
- 1 teaspoon maple flavored extract
- 2 cups semisweet chocolate chips

Directions

Step 1

Combine the butter, peanut butter, confectioners' sugar, vanilla and maple flavoring. Cream well and knead well.

Step 2

Melt the chocolate chips over low heat. Roll the dough into 1 inch balls. Dip into melted chocolate chips.

Step 3

Refrigerate overnight (or at least for about 15 minutes) on a cookie sheet lined with wax paper.

Nutrition Facts

Per Serving:

206.1 calories; protein 3.7g 7% DV; carbohydrates 25.6g 8% DV; fat 11.4g 18% DV; cholesterol 4.1mg 1% DV; sodium 71.5mg 3% DV.

Orange Drop Cookies II

Servings: 18 **Yield:** 3 dozen

Ingredients

- ⅔ cup shortening
- ¾ cup white sugar
- 1 egg
- ½ cup orange juice
- 1 teaspoon orange zest
- 2 cups all-purpose flour
- ½ teaspoon baking powder
- ½ teaspoon baking soda
- ½ teaspoon salt
- 2 cups confectioners' sugar
- 2 tablespoons butter
- 2 tablespoons orange juice
- 1 teaspoon orange zest

Directions

Step 1

Preheat oven to 350 degrees F (175 degrees C). Grease cookie sheets.

Step 2

Mix together flour, baking powder, baking soda and salt. Stir 1/2 cup orange juice and 1 teaspoon rind into the flour mixture.

Step 3

Cream shortening and white sugar together. Mix egg into the sugar mixture thoroughly. Slowly blend flour mixture into the egg and sugar mixture. Drop by teaspoonful onto greased cookie sheet.

Step 4

Bake for 8 to 10 minutes.

Step 5

Make the icing: Mix confectioner's sugar and 2 tablespoons butter together until smooth. Pour 2 tablespoons orange juice and 1 teaspoon orange rind into the sugar and butter mixture, mix well. When the cookies have cooled spread the icing generously over the tops of the cookies.

Nutrition Facts

Per Serving:

221.2 calories; protein 1.9g 4% DV; carbohydrates 33.2g 11% DV; fat 9.3g 14% DV; cholesterol 13.7mg 5% DV; sodium 126.6mg 5% DV.

Meringue Mushrooms

Prep: 45 mins **Cook:** 1 hr **Total:** 1 hr 45 mins **Servings:** 36 **Yield:** 36 mushrooms

Ingredients

- ½ cup egg whites
- ¼ teaspoon cream of tartar
- ¼ teaspoon salt
- 1 teaspoon vanilla extract
- 1 cup white sugar
- 1 tablespoon unsweetened cocoa powder
- 4 ounces chocolate confectioners' coating

Directions

Step 1

Preheat the oven to 225 degrees F (110 degrees C). Line 2 cookie sheets with parchment paper or aluminum foil.

Step 2

In a large glass or metal bowl, use an electric mixer to whip egg whites until foamy. Add cream of tartar, salt, and vanilla. Continue whipping until the whites hold soft peaks. Gradually sprinkle in the sugar so that it does not sink to the bottom, and continue whipping until the mixture holds stiff shiny peaks.

Step 3

Place a round tip into a pastry bag, and fill the bag half way with the meringue. To pipe the mushroom caps, squeeze out round mounds of meringue onto one of the prepared cookie sheets. Pull the bag off to the side to avoid making peaks on the top. For the stems, press out a tiny bit of meringue onto the other sheet, then pull the bag straight up. They should resemble candy kisses. Do not worry about making all of the pieces exactly the same. The mushrooms will look more natural if the pieces are different sizes. Dust the mushroom caps lightly with cocoa using a small sifter or strainer.

Step 4

Bake for 1 hour in the preheated oven, or until the caps are dry enough to easily remove from the cookie sheets. Set aside to cool completely. Melt the coating chocolate in a metal bowl over simmering water, or in a glass bowl in the microwave, stirring occasionally until smooth.

Step 5

Poke a small hole in the bottom of a mushroom cap. Spread chocolate over the bottom of the cap. Dip the tip of a stem in chocolate, and press lightly into the hole. When the chocolate sets, they will hold together. Repeat with remaining pieces. Store at room temperature in a dry place or tin.

Nutrition Facts

Per Serving:

38.7 calories; protein 0.6g 1% DV; carbohydrates 7.1g 2% DV; fat 1.3g 2% DV; cholesterolmg; sodium 21.9mg 1% DV.

Scandinavian Almond Bars

Prep: 10 mins **Cook:** 10 mins **Additional:** 10 mins **Total:** 30 mins **Servings:** 48 **Yield:** 4 dozen

Ingredients

- ½ cup butter
- 1 cup white sugar
- 1 egg
- ½ teaspoon almond extract
- 1 ¾ cups all-purpose flour
- 2 teaspoons baking powder

- ¼ teaspoon salt
- ½ cup sliced almonds
- 2 tablespoons milk
- 1 cup confectioners' sugar
- ¼ teaspoon almond extract
- ¼ cup milk

Directions

Step 1

Preheat oven to 325 degrees F (165 degrees C).

Step 2

In a medium bowl, cream butter and sugar. Add egg and almond extract; mix until fluffy. Stir in flour, baking powder and salt; mix well.

Step 3

Divide dough into 4 pieces, and roll each one into a log about 12 inches long. Place 2 logs per cookie sheet 4 to 5 inches apart. Flatten each roll by hand until it is about 3 inches wide. Brush flattened roll with milk and sprinkle with sliced almonds.

Step 4

Bake in preheated oven 12 to 15 minutes or until edges are slightly browned. While the cookies are still warm, cut them crosswise at a diagonal, into slices about 1 inch wide. When cool, drizzle with almond icing.

Step 5

Almond icing: In a small bowl, stir together powdered sugar, almond extract, and milk until smooth. Drizzle over the cookies.

Nutrition Facts

Per Serving:

67.7 calories; protein 0.9g 2% DV; carbohydrates 10.4g 3% DV; fat 2.6g 4% DV; cholesterol 9.1mg 3% DV; sodium 48.1mg 2% DV.

Italian Fig Cookies I

Servings: 60 Yield: 4 -5 dozen

Ingredients

- 2 cups shortening
- 3 cups white sugar
- 6 large eggs eggs
- 8 cups all-purpose flour
- 7 teaspoons baking powder
- 2 tablespoons vanilla extract
- 1 pinch salt
- 2 cups whole milk

- 4 pounds dried figs
- 1 pound raisins
- 2 teaspoons ground cinnamon
- ½ cup white sugar
- 1 whole orange, with peel
- 1 small apple
- 1 ½ cups chopped pecans
- 1 cup water

Directions

Step 1

To Make Dough: Cream sugar and shortening. Add eggs, vanilla, and salt. Blend in flour and baking powder by hand. Knead dough until smooth and workable. Add milk to reach workable consistency. (This takes a while and you will get a workout, but you'll know when it's right.)

Step 2

To Make Filling: Cut up figs, orange, and apple into small pieces. (It is easier to grind this way). Grind figs, raisins, orange, and apple. If the mixture is too dry or thick, mix in up to 1 cup of water, if desired. (I do not use the water, the juice from the apple and orange are enough). The spices and chopped nuts are added to the ground fig mixture. After the fig mixture is ground, I sprinkle them in over the mixture and mix (knead) it in by hand. STICKY! But good.

50

Step 3

Preheat oven to 375 degrees F (190 degrees C).

Step 4

Roll out some dough. (should be kind of thin). Put fig mixture in a line. Wrap dough over mixture, sealing figs inside dough. Trim to desired length, using a diagonal cut. Make small diagonal slits in the sides of the cookies. Bake on ungreased cookie sheet for 10-15 minutes. (Dough makes good cookies without the filling also). Wonderful with coffee.

Nutrition Facts

Per Serving:

301.5 calories; protein 4.1g 8% DV; carbohydrates 51.9g 17% DV; fat 10.1g 16% DV; cholesterol 19.4mg 7% DV; sodium 71.8mg 3% DV.

Caramel Filled Chocolate Cookies

Prep: 20 mins **Cook:** 10 mins **Additional:** 2 hrs 30 mins **Total:** 3 hrs **Servings:** 24 **Yield:** 4 dozen

Ingredients

- 1 cup butter, softened
- 1 cup white sugar
- 1 cup packed brown sugar
- 2 large eggs eggs
- 2 teaspoons vanilla extract
- 2 ¼ cups all-purpose flour
- 1 teaspoon baking soda
- ¾ cup unsweetened cocoa powder
- 1 cup chopped walnuts
- 1 tablespoon white sugar
- 48 piece (0.2 oz)s chocolate-covered caramel candies

Directions

Step 1

Beat butter until creamy. Gradually beat in white sugar and brown sugar. Beat in eggs and vanilla. Combine flour, baking soda, and cocoa. Gradually add to butter mixture, beating well. Stir in 1/2 cup walnuts. Cover and chill at least 2 hours.

Step 2

Preheat oven to 375 degrees F (190 degrees C).

Step 3

Combine remaining 1/2 cup nuts with the 1 tablespoon sugar. Divide the dough into 4 parts. Work with one part at a time, leaving the remainder in the refrigerator until needed. Divide each part into 12 pieces.

Quickly press each piece of dough around a chocolate covered caramel. Roll into a ball. Dip the tops into the sugar mixture. Place sugar side up, 2 inches apart on greased baking sheets.

Step 4

Bake for 8 minutes in the preheated oven. Let cool for 3 to 4 minutes on the baking sheets before removing to wire racks to cool completely.

Nutrition Facts

Per Serving:

253 calories; protein 3.4g 7% DV; carbohydrates 33.1g 11% DV; fat 13g 20% DV; cholesterol 36.6mg 12% DV; sodium 127.5mg 5% DV.

Cookie Mix in a Jar III

Prep: 20 mins **Total:** 20 mins **Servings:** 36 **Yield:** 3 dozen

Ingredients

- 1 cup all-purpose flour
- 1 teaspoon ground cinnamon
- ½ teaspoon ground nutmeg
- 1 teaspoon baking soda
- ½ teaspoon salt

- ¾ cup raisins
- 2 cups rolled oats
- ¾ cup packed brown sugar
- ½ cup white sugar

Directions

Step 1

Mix together flour, ground cinnamon, ground nutmeg, baking soda, and salt. Set aside.

Step 2

Layer ingredients in the following order into a 1 quart, wide mouth canning jar: Flour mixture, raisins, rolled oats, brown sugar, and white sugar. It will be a tight fit, make sure you firmly pack down each layer before adding the next layer.

Step 3

Attach a tag with the following instructions: Oatmeal Raisin Spice Cookies 1. Preheat oven to 350 degrees F (175 degrees C). Line cookie sheets with parchment paper. 2. Empty jar of cookie mix into large mixing bowl. Use your hands to thoroughly mix. 3. Mix in 3/4 cup butter or margarine, softened. Stir in one slightly beaten egg and 1 teaspoon of vanilla. Mix until completely blended. You will need to finish mixing with your hands. Shape into balls the size of walnuts. Place on a parchment lined cookie sheets 2 inches apart. 4. Bake for 11 to 13 minutes in preheated oven, or until edges are lightly browned. Cool 5 minutes on cookie sheet. Transfer cookies to wire racks to finish cooling.

Nutrition Facts

Per Serving:

67.3 calories; protein 1.1g 2% DV; carbohydrates 15.4g 5% DV; fat 0.4g 1% DV; cholesterolmg; sodium 69.2mg 3% DV.

Basic Sugar Cookies - Tried and True Since 1960

Prep: 30 mins **Cook:** 15 mins **Additional:** 2 hrs **Total:** 2 hrs 45 mins **Servings:** 48 **Yield:** 4 dozen cookies

Ingredients

- 3 cups self-rising flour
- 1 cup butter at room temperature
- 1 cup white sugar, or more to taste

- 2 large eggs eggs at room temperature
- 1 ½ teaspoons vanilla extract
- ¼ teaspoon salt

Directions

Step 1

Mix self-rising flour, butter, sugar, eggs, vanilla extract, and salt thoroughly in a bowl; beat at least 5 minutes. Refrigerate dough at least 2 hours to overnight.

Step 2

Preheat oven to 275 degrees F (135 degrees C).

Step 3

Roll dough out on a floured work surface using a lightly floured rolling pin; cut cookies out with cutters. Place cookies onto baking sheets.

Step 4

Bake in the preheated oven until cookie bottoms are lightly golden brown, about 15 minutes.

Nutrition Facts

Per Serving:

81.1 calories; protein 1.1g 2% DV; carbohydrates 10g 3% DV; fat 4.1g 6% DV; cholesterol 17.9mg 6% DV; sodium 141.5mg 6% DV.

Jam Kolaches

Prep: 45 mins **Cook:** 15 mins **Total:** 1 hr **Servings:** 12 **Yield:** 2 dozen

Ingredients

- ½ cup butter, softened
- 3 ounces cream cheese, softened
- 1 ¼ cups all-purpose flour
- ¼ cup strawberry jam
- ¼ cup sifted confectioners' sugar

Directions

Step 1

Beat butter and cream cheese in mixer bowl until light and fluffy. Add flour gradually, beating well after each addition.

Step 2

Roll dough to 1/8 inch thickness on lightly floured surface. Cut into 2-inch circles. Spoon 1/4 teaspoon jam into center of each circle. Fold opposite edges together, slightly overlapping edges.

Step 3

Place 2 inches apart on greased cookie sheet. Bake at 375 degrees F (190 degrees C) for 15 minutes. Remove to wire rack to cool. Sprinkle with confectioners' sugar.

Nutrition Facts

Per Serving:

167.8 calories; protein 2g 4% DV; carbohydrates 17.3g 6% DV; fat 10.3g 16% DV; cholesterol 28.1mg 9% DV; sodium 75.7mg 3% DV.

Pumpkin Cheesecake Bars

Prep: 25 mins **Cook:** 35 mins **Additional:** 30 mins **Total:** 1 hr 30 mins **Servings:** 24 **Yield:** 24 bars

Ingredients

- 1 (16 ounce) package pound cake mix
- 3 large eggs eggs
- 2 tablespoons butter, melted
- 4 teaspoons pumpkin pie spice
- 1 (8 ounce) package cream cheese, softened
- 1 (14 ounce) can sweetened condensed milk
- 1 (15 ounce) can pumpkin puree
- ½ teaspoon salt
- 1 cup chopped pecans

Directions

Step 1

Preheat oven to 350 degrees C (175 degrees C). Coat a 15x10 inch jelly roll pan with non-stick spray.

Step 2

In a large mixing bowl, on low speed, combine cake mix, 1 egg, margarine, and 2 teaspoons pumpkin pie spice until crumbly. Press onto bottom of prepared pan.

Step 3

In another large mixing bowl, beat cream cheese until fluffy. Gradually beat in sweetened condensed milk, then remaining two eggs, pumpkin, remaining 2 teaspoons pumpkin pie spice, and salt; mix well. Pour over crust; sprinkle with pecans.

Step 4

Bake 30 to 35 minutes, or until set.

Step 5

Cool, then chill in refrigerator. Cut into squares. Store covered in refrigerator.

Nutrition Facts

Per Serving:

232.8 calories; protein 4.5g 9% DV; carbohydrates 24g 8% DV; fat 13.9g 21% DV; cholesterol 52.3mg 17% DV; sodium 226.8mg 9% DV.

Chocolate Balls

Prep: 20 mins **Additional:** 15 mins **Total:** 35 mins **Servings:** 36 **Yield:** 3 dozen

Ingredients

- 1 cup peanut butter
- ¾ cup confectioners' sugar
- 1 cup graham cracker crumbs
- 2 cups semisweet chocolate chips
- 3 (1 ounce) squares semisweet chocolate, chopped
- 1 tablespoon shortening

Directions

Step 1

In a medium bowl, mix together the peanut butter and confectioners' sugar until smooth. Stir in graham cracker crumbs until well blended. Form the dough into 1 inch balls by rolling in your hands, or by using a cookie scoop.

Step 2

Melt the semisweet chocolate chips, semisweet chocolate squares, and the shortening in the top half of a double boiler. Use a fork to dip the balls into the melted chocolate, and place on wax paper to cool until set.

Nutrition Facts

Per Serving:

121.3 calories; protein 2.5g 5% DV; carbohydrates 12.9g 4% DV; fat 7.8g 12% DV; cholesterolmg; sodium 48.1mg 2% DV.

My Grandma's Fruitcake Cookies

Prep: 20 mins **Cook:** 25 mins **Additional:** 45 mins **Total:** 1 hr 30 mins **Servings:** 144 **Yield:** 12 dozen cookies

Ingredients

- 3 cups all-purpose flour
- 1 teaspoon ground cinnamon
- ½ teaspoon baking soda
- 1 cup butter, at room temperature
- 1 cup brown sugar, packed
- 3 large eggs eggs
- ½ cup milk
- 2 tablespoons vanilla-flavored cream sherry
- 7 cups chopped mixed nuts
- 2 cups chopped raisins
- 2 cups pitted chopped dates

- 1 pound candied pineapple, coarsely chopped
- 1 pound red and green candied cherries, chopped

Directions

Step 1

Preheat oven to 300 degrees F (150 degrees C). Grease several baking sheets. Sift together the flour, cinnamon, and baking soda in a bowl; set aside.

Step 2

Beat together the butter and brown sugar in a large mixing bowl until fluffy, about 5 minutes. Beat in the eggs, one at a time. Gradually beat the flour mixture into the butter mixture, alternating each addition with about 2 tablespoons of milk until all the milk is incorporated and the dough is soft. Beat in the sherry, and mix in the nuts, raisins, dates, pineapple, and cherries until thoroughly mixed. Drop the dough by rounded teaspoons onto the prepared baking sheets.

Step 3

Bake in the preheated oven until the cookies are set and the bottoms are very lightly browned, 20 to 30 minutes. Cool on wire racks.

Nutrition Facts

Per Serving:

99.6 calories; protein 1.7g 3% DV; carbohydrates 12.4g 4% DV; fat 5.3g 8% DV; cholesterol 7.3mg 2% DV; sodium 20.9mg 1% DV.

Traditional Swedish Pepparkakor

Prep: 30 mins **Cook:** 5 mins **Additional:** 1 hr **Total:** 1 hr 35 mins **Servings:** 100 **Yield:** 100 servings

Ingredients

- 3 ¾ cups all-purpose flour
- 2 teaspoons baking soda
- 1 teaspoon cinnamon
- 1 teaspoon ground cloves
- 1 teaspoon ground ginger
- 1 teaspoon ground cardamom
- 1 cup butter
- 1 cup white sugar
- ½ cup brown sugar, packed
- 1 egg, beaten
- 2 tablespoons dark corn syrup

Directions

Step 1

Sift the flour together with the baking soda, cinnamon, cloves, ginger, and cardamom in a mixing bowl.

Step 2

Beat the butter together with the white and brown sugars in a mixing bowl until light and fluffy. Mix in the egg and corn syrup until smooth. Gradually stir in the flour mixture until evenly blended. Divide the dough into 4 equal portions and wrap tightly each with plastic wrap. Refrigerate at least 1 hour, or overnight.

Step 3

Preheat oven to 375 degrees F (190 degrees C). Lightly grease baking sheets.

Step 4

Using 1 portion at a time, work on a floured surface and roll out dough to 1/8 inch thick. Cut into shapes with cookie cutter, and place 1 inch apart on prepared baking sheets.

Step 5

Bake in preheated oven until set, about 5 minutes. Cool completely. Store in tightly covered tins.

Nutrition Facts

Per Serving:

47.4 calories; protein 0.9g 2% DV; carbohydrates 7g 2% DV; fat 1.9g 3% DV; cholesterol 6.7mg 2% DV; sodium 39.9mg 2% DV.

Chocolate-Dipped Orange Shortbread Cookies

Prep: 30 mins **Cook:** 20 mins **Additional:** 1 hr **Total:** 1 hr 50 mins **Servings:** 36 **Yield:** 36 servings

Ingredients

- 2 ½ cups all-purpose flour
- ⅓ cup white sugar
- 3 tablespoons orange zest, divided
- ½ teaspoon ground cinnamon
- ⅛ teaspoon ground nutmeg
- ⅛ teaspoon ground cloves
- 1 cup butter, softened
- 2 tablespoons milk
- 4 ounces milk chocolate, melted

Directions

Step 1

Combine flour, sugar, 2 tablespoons orange zest, cinnamon, nutmeg, and cloves in the bowl of a stand mixer fitted with the paddle attachment. Add butter and beat until mixture resembles crumbs and starts to stick together. Work until dough sticks together and forms a smooth ball that is not sticky, adding milk if mixture is too dry. Press into a disk shape and wrap in wax paper. Chill in the refrigerator for 30 minutes

Step 2

Preheat the oven to 325 degrees F (165 degrees C). Line 2 baking sheets with parchment paper.

Step 3

Lightly flour a clean countertop. Roll dough to 1/2-inch thickness. Cut into shapes with cookie cutters and place on the prepared baking sheets.

Step 4

Bake cookies in the preheated oven until bottoms are lightly golden, 18 to 22 minutes. Transfer cookies to wire racks and cool completely, about 30 minutes.

Step 5

Line the countertop with wax paper. Dip tops of cookies into the melted chocolate, allowing excess to drip back into the bowl. Place cookies on the wax paper and immediately sprinkle tops with remaining 1 tablespoon orange zest. Let dry.

Nutrition Facts

Per Serving:

101.7 calories; protein 1.2g 3% DV; carbohydrates 10.5g 3% DV; fat 6.1g 10% DV; cholesterol 14.3mg 5% DV; sodium 39.3mg 2% DV.

Traditional Springerle

Prep: 10 mins **Cook:** 25 mins **Additional:** 8 hrs **Total:** 8 hrs 35 mins **Servings:** 48 **Yield:** 48 servings

Ingredients

- 1 ½ tablespoons crushed anise seeds
- 3 ½ cups all-purpose flour
- 1 teaspoon baking powder
- 4 large eggs eggs
- 2 cups sugar
- ½ teaspoon vanilla extract
- ¼ cup confectioners' sugar

Directions

Step 1

Lightly grease 4 cookie sheets. Sprinkle with anise seeds. Set aside until needed.

Step 2

Mix the flour and baking powder together in a bowl until well blended. Place the eggs, sugar, and vanilla in a large bowl; beat until light and frothy, 5 to 8 minutes. Slowly stir in the flour mixture until a thick dough forms.

Step 3

Working with handfuls of dough, roll out the dough onto a lightly floured surface until 1/4 inch thick. Lightly sift confectioners' sugar over the dough. Place springerle molds onto the dough; press down hard and evenly until the mold's design registers in the dough. Remove the mold. Use a small knife to cut around each cookie, and place on prepared cookie sheets. Repeat, until all dough has been used. Cover the cookies with a lightweight cotton cloth, and allow to dry 8 hours, or overnight.

Step 4

Preheat oven to 250 degrees F (120 degrees C).

Step 5

Bake cookies in preheated oven until tops are pale brown and set, 25 to 30 minutes. Cool on a rack. Store in an airtight container.

Nutrition Facts

Per Serving:

74.8 calories; protein 1.5g 3% DV; carbohydrates 16.1g 5% DV; fat 0.5g 1% DV; cholesterol 15.5mg 5% DV; sodium 16.2mg 1% DV.

Christmas Cornflake Wreath Cookies

Servings: 18 **Yield:** 3 dozen

Ingredients

- ½ cup butter
- 4 cups miniature marshmallows
- 1 teaspoon green food coloring
- ½ teaspoon almond extract
- ½ teaspoon vanilla extract
- 4 cups cornflakes cereal
- 1 (2.25 ounce) package cinnamon red hot candies

Directions

Step 1

Microwave marshmallows and butter on High for 2 minutes. Stir, then microwave on High for 2 minutes more. Stir. (This can be done in a double boiler if one doesn't have a microwave.)

Step 2

Add and mix quickly the coloring, extracts, then cornflakes. Drop by spoonfuls in clumps on greased wax paper and decorate with 3 red hots each.

Step 3

Once cool, transfer to lightly greased serving/storage tray with lightly greased fingers.

Nutrition Facts

Per Serving:

117.5 calories; protein 0.7g 1% DV; carbohydrates 17.9g 6% DV; fat 5.2g 8% DV; cholesterol 13.6mg 5% DV; sodium 91.5mg 4% DV.

Brownie Mix in a Jar II

Prep: 20 mins **Total:** 20 mins **Servings:** 24 **Yield:** 2 dozen

Ingredients

- 1 ¼ cups all-purpose flour
- 1 teaspoon baking powder
- 1 teaspoon salt
- ⅔ cup unsweetened cocoa powder
- 2 ¼ cups white sugar
- ½ cup chopped pecans

Directions

Step 1

Mix together flour, baking powder, and salt in a quart jar. Layer remaining ingredients in the order listed. Press each layer firmly in place before adding the next layer. NOTE: Be sure to wipe out the inside of the jar with a dry paper towel after adding the cocoa powder, so the other layers will show through the glass.

Step 2

Attach a tag with the following instructions: Brownie Mix in a Jar 1. Preheat the oven to 350 degrees F (175 degrees C). Grease and flour a 9x13inch baking pan. 2. Empty jar of brownie mix into a large mixing bowl, and stir to blend. Mix in 3/4 cup melted butter and 4 eggs. Mix thoroughly. Spread batter evenly into prepared baking pan. 3. Bake for 25 to 30 minutes in preheated oven. Cool completely in pan before cutting into 2 inch squares.

Nutrition Facts

Per Serving:

117.5 calories; protein 1.3g 3% DV; carbohydrates 25.4g 8% DV; fat 2g 3% DV; cholesterolmg; sodium 117.8mg 5% DV.

Shortbread Cookies III

Servings: 24 **Yield:** 4 dozen

Ingredients

- 1 ½ cups butter, softened
- 2 cups all-purpose flour
- 1 cup confectioners' sugar
- 1 cup cornstarch
- ¼ teaspoon salt

Directions

Step 1

Work all the ingredients together with your hands until blended. Shape all of the dough into 1 inch balls.

Step 2

Bake cookies on ungreased cookie sheets, 2 inches apart at 300 degrees F (150 degrees C) for 20 minutes.

Step 3

Let cool 10 minutes then carefully lift with spatula to cake racks to cool. Store in air tight container with wax paper between layers. Cookies keep well.

Step 4

Variations: Flatten some balls with tines of fork and press 1/4 of a red or green glace cherry in center of each. Make thumbprint indentation in some balls and fill with a tiny bit of jam, jelly or marmalade. Dip some balls in slightly beaten egg white and roll in finely chopped walnuts. Bake as they are or make an indentation in top and spoon in a little jam or marmalade. Dip some balls in egg white and roll in desiccated coconut. Bake as they are or make an indentation and spoon in a little jam, jelly or marmalade.

Nutrition Facts

Per Serving:

179.4 calories; protein 1.2g 2% DV; carbohydrates 17.8g 6% DV; fat 11.6g 18% DV; cholesterol 30.5mg 10% DV; sodium 106.7mg 4% DV.

Christmas Wreaths

Prep: 5 mins **Cook:** 10 mins **Additional:** 15 mins **Total:** 30 mins **Servings:** 18 **Yield:** 1 1/2 dozen

Ingredients

- ½ cup butter
- 30 regulars large marshmallows
- 1 ½ teaspoons green food coloring
- 1 teaspoon vanilla extract
- 4 cups cornflakes cereal
- 2 tablespoons cinnamon red hot candies

Directions

Step 1

Melt butter in a large saucepan over low heat. Add marshmallows, and cook until melted, stirring constantly. Remove from heat, and stir in the food coloring, vanilla, and cornflakes.

Step 2

Quickly drop heaping tablespoonfuls of the mixture onto waxed paper, and form into a wreath shape with lightly greased fingers. Immediately decorate with red hot candies. Allow to cool to room temperature before removing from waxed paper, and storing in an airtight container.

Nutrition Facts

Per Serving:

112.4 calories; protein 0.7g 1% DV; carbohydrates 16.7g 5% DV; fat 5.2g 8% DV; cholesterol 13.6mg 5% DV; sodium 91.5mg 4% DV.

Old Fashioned Butter Cookies with Butter Frosting

Prep: 30 mins **Cook:** 5 mins **Additional:** 2 hrs 30 mins **Total:** 3 hrs 5 mins **Servings:** 72 **Yield:** 6 dozen cookies

Ingredients

- 1 cup butter, softened
- ¾ cup white sugar
- 1 egg

- 2 tablespoons whole milk
- 1 ½ teaspoons vanilla extract
- 3 cups all-purpose flour

- 1 teaspoon baking powder
- ½ teaspoon salt

Frosting:

- 1 cup butter, softened
- 3 cups confectioners' sugar
- 1 ½ tablespoons vanilla extract
- 9 tablespoons evaporated milk, or more as needed
- 6 cups confectioners' sugar, or more as needed

Directions

Step 1

Beat 1 cup softened butter with white sugar in a large bowl until creamy. Beat egg, whole milk, and 1 1/2 teaspoons vanilla extract into butter mixture until smooth. Whisk flour, baking powder, and salt in a separate bowl and gradually stir dry ingredients into moist ingredients to make a smooth dough. Chill dough in refrigerator for 2 to 3 hours.

Step 2

Preheat oven to 400 degrees F (200 degrees C). Dust a pastry cloth or kitchen towel generously with flour.

Step 3

Divide dough into thirds and roll each third out 1/8-inch thick on the prepared pastry cloth. Cut shapes out of the rolled dough with cookie cutters. Place cookies onto ungreased baking sheets.

Step 4

Bake in the preheated oven until cookies are barely browned, 5 to 8 minutes. Let cookies cool on baking sheets for 5 minutes before removing to finish cooling on a wire rack.

Step 5

Beat 1 cup softened butter, 3 cups confectioners' sugar, 1 1/2 tablespoons vanilla extract, and evaporated milk in a bowl until smooth. Gradually stir 6 cups confectioners' sugar into mixture until combined. Beat frosting hard until fluffy; stir in additional evaporated milk or confectioners' sugar if needed to reach desired consistency. Frost cooled cookies.

Nutrition Facts

Per Serving:

135.5 calories; protein 0.8g 2% DV; carbohydrates 21.3g 7% DV; fat 5.4g 8% DV; cholesterol 16.8mg 6% DV; sodium 62.7mg 3% DV.

Nanaimo Bars I

Servings: 12 **Yield:** 2 dozen

Ingredients

- ½ cup butter
- ¼ cup white sugar
- 5 tablespoons unsweetened cocoa powder
- 1 egg
- 1 teaspoon vanilla extract
- 2 cups graham cracker crumbs
- 1 cup shredded coconut
- ½ cup chopped walnuts

- ¼ cup butter
- 2 cups confectioners' sugar
- 2 tablespoons vanilla custard powder
- 3 tablespoons milk
- 4 (1 ounce) squares semisweet chocolate, chopped
- 1 tablespoon butter

Directions

Step 1

Mix 1/2 cup butter or margarine, white sugar, cocoa, egg and vanilla in a heavy sauce pan or double boiler. Stir over low heat until mixture is of custard like consistency.

Step 2

Combine graham crackers, coconut and walnuts and add to the melted mixture. Mix well and pack into buttered 9 inch square cake pan.

Step 3

Cream 1/4 cup butter, confectioners' sugar, vanilla custard powder and milk. Beat until creamy and spread over melted base.

Step 4

Refrigerate till hardened.

Step 5

Melt semi-sweet chocolate with 1 tablespoon butter and drizzle over custard icing. Refrigerate. When totally hard cut into square bars.

Nutrition Facts

Per Serving:

389.2 calories; protein 3.8g 8% DV; carbohydrates 46.8g 15% DV; fat 22.6g 35% DV; cholesterol 48.9mg 16% DV; sodium 199mg 8% DV.

Chocolate Brittle Surprise

Servings: 12 **Yield:** 2 dozen

Ingredients

- 35 crackers unsalted soda crackers
- 1 cup butter
- 1 cup packed brown sugar
- 2 cups semisweet chocolate chips
- 1 cup chopped pecans

Directions

Step 1

Preheat oven to 350 degrees F (180 degrees C). Cover cookie sheet with foil. Spray foil with cooking oil spray.

Step 2

Place crackers on foil in 5 x 7 inch rows.

Step 3

Microwave butter on high for 2 minutes. Add brown sugar and stir. Microwave on high for 2 more minutes, stirring every 30 seconds.

Step 4

Pour over crackers. Bake 17 - 20 minutes (should bubble but not burn).

Step 5

Sprinkle chocolate chips over hot crackers. Spread after 2 minutes (chips have softened). Sprinkle nuts on top.

Step 6

Refrigerate 1 hour. Break into pieces. Can be frozen.

Nutrition Facts

Per Serving:

440.2 calories; protein 3g 6% DV; carbohydrates 43.2g 14% DV; fat 31.3g 48% DV; cholesterol 40.7mg 14% DV; sodium 184.2mg 7% DV.

Grandma's Drop Sugar Cookies

Prep: 10 mins **Cook:** 10 mins **Total:** 20 mins **Servings:** 48 **Yield:** 4 dozen cookies

Ingredients

- 2 cups white sugar
- 2 cups butter, softened
- 3 cups all-purpose flour
- 1 cup coconut flakes
- 1 teaspoon vanilla extract
- 1 teaspoon salt
- ½ teaspoon baking soda

Directions

Step 1

Preheat oven to 350 degrees F (175 degrees C).

Step 2

Beat sugar and butter together in a bowl using an electric mixer until smooth and creamy. Mix flour, coconut flakes, vanilla extract, salt, and baking soda into creamed butter mixture until dough is smooth. Spoon dough onto a baking sheet.

Step 3

Bake in the preheated oven until edges of cookies are lightly browned, about 10 minutes.

Nutrition Facts

Per Serving:

135.8 calories; protein 0.9g 2% DV; carbohydrates 15.1g 5% DV; fat 8.2g 13% DV; cholesterol 20.3mg 7% DV; sodium 120.6mg 5% DV.

McCormick Gingerbread Men Cookies

Prep: 20 mins **Cook:** 10 mins **Additional:** 4 hrs **Total:** 4 hrs 30 mins **Servings:** 24 **Yield:** 24 (1 cookie) servings

Ingredients

- 3 cups flour
- 2 teaspoons McCormick Ground Ginger
- 1 teaspoon McCormick Ground Cinnamon
- 1 teaspoon baking soda
- ¼ teaspoon McCormick Ground Nutmeg
- ¼ teaspoon salt
- ¾ cup butter, softened
- ¾ cup firmly packed brown sugar
- ½ cup molasses
- 1 egg

- 1 teaspoon McCormick Pure Vanilla Extract

Directions

Step 1

Mix flour, ginger, cinnamon, baking soda, nutmeg and salt in large bowl. Beat butter and brown sugar in another large bowl with electric mixer on medium speed until light and fluffy. Add molasses, egg and vanilla; beat well. Gradually beat in flour mixture on low speed until well mixed. Press dough into a thick flat disk. Wrap in plastic wrap. Refrigerate 4 hours or overnight.

Step 2

Preheat oven to 350 degrees F. Roll out dough to 1/4-inch thickness on lightly floured work surface. Cut into gingerbread men shapes with 5-inch cookie cutter. Place 1 inch apart on ungreased baking sheets.

Step 3

Bake 8 to 10 minutes or until edges of cookies are set and just begin to brown. Cool on baking sheets 1 to 2 minutes. Remove to wire racks; cool completely. Decorate cooled cookies as desired. Store cookies in airtight container up to 5 days.

Nutrition Facts

Per Serving:

158.1 calories; protein 2g 4% DV; carbohydrates 24g 8% DV; fat 6.1g 10% DV; cholesterol 23mg 8% DV; sodium 125.3mg 5% DV.

Rum Balls

Prep: 20 mins **Cook:** 5 mins **Additional:** 45 mins **Total:** 1 hr 10 mins **Servings:** 24 **Yield:** 2 dozen rum balls

Ingredients

- 1 (12 ounce) box vanilla wafer cookies (such as Nilla)
- 1 cup semisweet chocolate chips
- ¼ cup light corn syrup
- ¾ cup dark rum (such as Meyer's)
- 1 cup confectioners' sugar, plus more for dusting

Directions

Step 1

Place vanilla cookies in a food processor and process into fine crumbs.

Step 2

Heat chocolate chips and corn syrup together in a saucepan over low heat. Cook, stirring often, until chocolate is melted and smooth, about 5 minutes. Remove from heat and stir in rum and confectioners' sugar until smooth. Fold in cookie crumbs; dough will be sticky.

Step 3

Place saucepan in the refrigerator until dough is firm and easy to roll, about 15 minutes. Cover 2 plates with waxed paper; dust with confectioners' sugar.

Step 4

Roll dough into 1-inch balls and place on the prepared plates. Dust rum balls with confectioners' sugar. Refrigerate until firm, about 30 minutes.

Step 5

Remove rum balls from refrigerator and transfer to a resealable bag, including the extra confectioners' sugar. Seal the bag and shake to coat the rum balls completely with confectioners' sugar.

Nutrition Facts

Per Serving:

147.6 calories; protein 0.9g 2% DV; carbohydrates 22.3g 7% DV; fat 4.9g 8% DV; cholesterolmg; sodium 46.4mg 2% DV.

My Favorite Sugar Cookies

Prep: 30 mins **Cook:** 8 mins **Additional:** 2 hrs **Total:** 2 hrs 38 mins **Servings:** 12 **Yield:** 6 dozen

Ingredients

- 1 ½ cups white sugar
- ⅔ cup shortening
- 2 large eggs eggs
- 2 tablespoons milk
- 1 teaspoon vanilla extract

- 3 ¼ cups all-purpose flour
- 2 ½ teaspoons baking powder
- ½ teaspoon salt
- 1 egg white

Directions

Step 1

Combine sugar and shortening in a mixing bowl. Beat at low speed just until smooth. Mix in eggs, milk, and vanilla.

Step 2

In separate bowl, whisk flour, baking soda and salt. Pour into sugar mixture and blend until combined.

Step 3

Shape dough into a ball and wrap with waxed paper or plastic wrap. Refrigerate 2 to 3 hours until easy to handle.

Step 4

Preheat oven to 400 degrees F (200 degrees C). Lightly grease cookie sheets or line them with parchment paper.

Step 5

Roll out half of the dough at a time on a lightly floured surface. Keep the remaining dough refrigerated. For crisp cookies, roll paper-thin. For softer cookies, roll 1/8 to 1/4 inch thick.

Step 6

With floured cookie cutters, cut dough into various shapes. Re-roll dough trimmings into a ball, cover and refrigerate, and continue to cut shapes with chilled dough.

Step 7

Place cookies 1/2 inch apart on greased cookie sheets. To glaze, brush tops of cookies with heavy or whipping cream or with an egg white slightly beaten with 1 tablespoon of water.

Step 8

Sprinkle cookies with your choice of toppings; bake 8 minutes or until very light brown. Remove cookies and cool completely.

Nutrition Facts

Per Serving:

336.7 calories; protein 4.9g 10% DV; carbohydrates 51.3g 17% DV; fat 12.6g 19% DV; cholesterol 31.2mg 10% DV; sodium 216.5mg 9% DV.

Dish Pan Cookies

Prep: 15 mins **Cook:** 1 hr 30 mins **Total:** 1 hr 45 mins **Servings:** 60 **Yield:** 12 dozen

Ingredients

- 2 cups white sugar
- 2 cups light brown sugar

- 4 large eggs eggs
- 2 cups vegetable oil
- 2 teaspoons vanilla extract
- 4 cups all-purpose flour
- 2 teaspoons baking soda
- 2 teaspoons salt
- 4 cups cornflakes cereal
- 1 ½ cups rolled oats
- 1 cup flaked coconut
- 1 cup chopped pecans
- 1 cup chopped dates
- 1 cup raisins

Directions

Step 1

Preheat oven to 325 degrees F (165 degrees C). Lightly grease a cookie sheet.

Step 2

Cream white sugar, brown sugar, eggs, vegetable oil and vanilla together in a large bowl or dishpan. In a separate bowl combine flour, baking soda and salt. Stir the flour mixture into the creamed sugar; mix until well combined.

Step 3

Stir corn flakes, oats, coconut, pecans, dates and raisins into the dough. You will most likely need to use your hands to mix everything thoroughly. Shape the dough into 1 1/2 to 2 inch balls and press them down lightly onto a greased cookie sheet.

Step 4

Bake in a preheated 325 degrees F (165 degrees C) oven for 10 to 14 minutes or until golden.

Nutrition Facts

Per Serving:

205.7 calories; protein 2.1g 4% DV; carbohydrates 27.3g 9% DV; fat 10.4g 16% DV; cholesterol 14.1mg 5% DV; sodium 140.3mg 6% DV.

Rum or Bourbon Balls

Prep: 10 mins **Cook:** 2 mins **Additional:** 1 week **Total:** 1 week **Servings:** 24 **Yield:** 4 dozen

Ingredients

- 1 cup semisweet chocolate chips
- ½ cup white sugar
- 3 tablespoons corn syrup
- ½ cup rum
- 2 ½ cups crushed vanilla wafers
- 1 cup chopped walnuts
- ⅓ cup confectioners' sugar

Directions

Step 1

Place chocolate chips into a microwave-safe medium bowl. Heat in the microwave for 1 minute, stir and then continue to heat at 20 second intervals, stirring between each, until melted and smooth. Stir in sugar and corn syrup. Blend in rum. Add crushed vanilla wafers and chopped nuts. Mix until evenly distributed. Cover and refrigerate until firm.

Step 2

Roll the chilled chocolate mixture into bite-size balls. Roll balls in a mixture of ground nuts and confectioner's sugar, or just plain confectioner's sugar. Store in a covered container for a week before serving to blend the flavors.

Nutrition Facts

Per Serving:

194.1 calories; protein 1.8g 4% DV; carbohydrates 26g 8% DV; fat 8.9g 14% DV; cholesterolmg; sodium 58.4mg 2% DV.

Apricot Cookies

Servings: 24 **Yield:** 4 dozen

Ingredients

- 1 cup butter
- 1 cup white sugar
- 3 cups all-purpose flour
- 1 teaspoon baking powder
- ½ teaspoon salt
- 1 egg
- 1 teaspoon vanilla extract
- 1 cup apricot preserves
- ⅓ cup confectioners' sugar for decoration

Directions

Step 1

Preheat oven to 350 degrees F (175 degrees C).

Step 2

Cream the butter and sugar in a medium size mixing bowl. Mix flour, baking powder, salt, egg and vanilla extract into the butter-sugar mixture. Cool dough in the refrigerator for 1 hour.

Step 3

On a lightly floured surface roll dough out to 1/4 inch thick. Cut the dough into rounds with a round cookie cutter or glass. Using the tip of a teaspoon place a small drop of apricot preserves into the middle of the circle. Brush edges with water and fold the dough over so that the cookie is in the shape of a half moon; seal edges Arrange on ungreased cookie sheets.

Step 4

Bake for 8 to 12 minutes, or until golden brown. Dust the cookies with powdered sugar while still hot.

Nutrition Facts

Per Serving:

202.4 calories; protein 2g 4% DV; carbohydrates 31.2g 10% DV; fat 8g 12% DV; cholesterol 28.1mg 9% DV; sodium 126.5mg 5% DV.

Caramel Turtles Brownies

Prep: 20 mins **Cook:** 30 mins **Total:** 50 mins **Servings:** 24 **Yield:** 24 servings

Ingredients

- 1 (14 ounce) package individually wrapped caramels
- 1 (12 fluid ounce) can evaporated milk
- 1 (18.25 ounce) package chocolate cake mix
- 6 tablespoons butter, melted
- 1 cup semisweet chocolate chips
- ¼ pound whole pecans

Directions

Step 1

Preheat oven to 350 degrees F (175 degrees C). Grease a 9x13 inch pan. Set aside.

Step 2

Unwrap caramels and place in saucepan with 2 Tablespoons evaporated milk. Melt over medium to low heat, stirring constantly.

Step 3

In a large bowl, combine the remaining evaporated milk, dry cake mix, and melted butter. Stir until well blended. Spread half of this mixture in the prepared pan. Bake for 10 minutes.

Step 4

Remove brownies from oven. Sprinkle chocolate chips and drizzle melted caramels over the top. Drop remaining cake mixture by teaspoonfuls over all. Return to oven for 20 minutes. Garnish with whole pecans if you'd like.

Nutrition Facts

Per Serving:

267.4 calories; protein 3.9g 8% DV; carbohydrates 35g 11% DV; fat 14.3g 22% DV; cholesterol 13.3mg 4% DV; sodium 255.6mg 10% DV.

Almond Crescent Cookies

Prep: 45 mins **Cook:** 15 mins **Total:** 1 hr **Servings:** 24 **Yield:** 2 dozen cookies

Ingredients

- ½ cup salted butter, at room temperature
- ⅓ cup confectioners' sugar, plus extra for dusting
- 1 teaspoon vanilla extract
- 1 teaspoon almond extract

- ⅛ teaspoon salt
- ¾ cup all-purpose flour, sifted
- 2 tablespoons all-purpose flour, sifted
- ½ cup almonds, finely chopped

Directions

Step 1

Preheat oven to 325 degrees F (165 degrees C).

Step 2

Beat butter and confectioners' sugar in a bowl using an electric mixer until smooth and creamy. Add vanilla extract, almond extract, and salt; mix briefly to incorporate. Gradually stir 3/4 cup plus 2 tablespoons flour into the creamed butter, add almonds, and mix until dough is just combined.

Step 3

Shape dough into tiny crescents; place on an ungreased baking sheet about 2 inches apart.

Step 4

Bake cookies in preheated oven until edges are golden, about 15 minutes. Cool on the baking sheet for 5 minutes before transferring to a wire rack to cool completely.

Step 5

Roll cookies in sifted confectioners' sugar when cooled.

Nutrition Facts

Per Serving:

69.7 calories; protein 0.9g 2% DV; carbohydrates 5.6g 2% DV; fat 4.9g 8% DV; cholesterol 10.2mg 3% DV; sodium 39.5mg 2% DV.

Anise Walnut Biscotti

Prep: 20 mins **Cook:** 25 mins **Additional:** 25 mins **Total:** 1 hr 10 mins **Servings:** 60 **Yield:** 5 dozen

Ingredients

- 1 cup butter, room temperature
- 2 ½ cups white sugar
- 2 teaspoons vanilla extract
- 8 large eggs eggs
- 7 teaspoons baking powder
- 8 cups all-purpose flour
- 2 teaspoons anise extract
- 3 teaspoons anise seed
- 1 cup chopped walnuts
- 2 large egg yolks egg yolks, lightly beaten

Directions

Step 1

Preheat oven to 375 degrees F (190 degrees C).

Step 2

In a large bowl, cream together butter and sugar Gradually add the vanilla and eggs while mixing. Sift together the flour and baking powder; stir into the egg mixture. For plain biscotti, do not add anything else (see Cook's Note). Stir in the anise extract and anise seed. Add walnuts if desired.

Step 3

Wet or grease your hands and shape dough out into 4 logs as long as your baking sheet will allow. Pat each one to about 3/4 inch in height, and 3 inches wide. Brush with beaten egg yolks.

Step 4

Bake in the preheated oven for 15 minutes, until golden brown. Slice logs at an angle, cutting pieces into 1/2 to 3/4-inch wide cookies. Place slices back onto the cookie sheet, standing upright, if possible; leave a gap between the slices. Return to the oven and bake until cookies are dry and lightly toasted, about 10 minutes more.

Nutrition Facts

Per Serving:

145.5 calories; protein 3g 6% DV; carbohydrates 21.6g 7% DV; fat 5.3g 8% DV; cholesterol 39.8mg 13% DV; sodium 88.7mg 4% DV.

Christmas Pinwheel Cookies

Prep: 25 mins **Cook:** 5 mins **Additional:** 8 hrs **Total:** 8 hrs 30 mins **Servings:** 72 **Yield:** 72 servings

Ingredients

- 4 cups all-purpose flour
- 1 teaspoon baking powder
- ¼ teaspoon baking soda
- 1 teaspoon salt
- 1 ⅓ cups butter
- 1 cup packed brown sugar

- ⅔ cup white sugar
- 2 large eggs eggs, beaten
- 1 ½ teaspoons vanilla extract
- 1 drop red food coloring, or as needed
- 1 drop green food coloring, or as needed

Directions

Step 1

Sift the flour, baking powder, baking soda, and salt together into a bowl. Resift again into another bowl.

Step 2

Beat the butter with the brown and white sugars in a mixing bowl until light and fluffy. Beat in the eggs and vanilla until smooth. Gradually stir in the flour mixture until evenly blended. Gather the dough into a ball, and divide into two equal parts. Place one half in a second bowl. Add red food coloring to the dough in one bowl, and green food coloring to the dough in the other bowl. Use a fork or wooden spoon to blend the food coloring into the dough until evenly blended. Add additional drops of food coloring to make the desired shade.

Step 3

Roll out the red dough to 1/4 inch (5mm) thickness. Roll out the green dough to 1/4 inch (5mm) thickness, and place on top of the red dough. Beginning on one edge, roll the doughs to make a log so the two colors spiral inside each other. Wrap the log in waxed paper, then in a cotton towel, and refrigerate at least 8 hours.

Step 4

Preheat oven to 400 degrees F (200 degrees C). Lightly grease 2 baking sheets.

Step 5

Unwrap the dough log, and place on a clean, lightly floured surface. Slice the log into rounds 1/8 inch (3 mm) thick, and place on prepared baking sheets.

Step 6

Bake in preheated oven until set, 5 to 6 minutes. Watch carefully to prevent edges from browning. Remove from oven, and cool on racks.

Nutrition Facts

Per Serving:

76.5 calories; protein 0.9g 2% DV; carbohydrates 10.2g 3% DV; fat 3.6g 6% DV; cholesterol 14.2mg 5% DV; sodium 70.6mg 3% DV.

Date Turnovers

Prep: 45 mins **Cook:** 15 mins **Additional:** 1 hr 40 mins **Total:** 2 hrs 40 mins **Servings:** 12 **Yield:** 2 dozen

Ingredients

- 2 cups pitted dates, chopped
- ½ cup water
- ¼ cup brown sugar
- 1 tablespoon cider vinegar
- ½ cup milk
- 2 cups all-purpose flour

- 1 teaspoon baking soda
- 2 ½ cups regular rolled oats
- 1 ½ cups brown sugar
- ½ cup melted butter
- ½ cup butter-flavored shortening (such as Crisco), melted

Directions

Step 1

Heat dates, water, and 1/4 cup brown sugar in a saucepan over medium heat; cook until dates are very soft, about 5 minutes. Set aside to cool to room temperature.

Step 2

Stir vinegar into milk in a bowl; set aside to curdle, about 10 minutes.

Step 3

Whisk flour and baking soda together in a large bowl; stir in oats and 1 1/2 cups brown sugar. Stir butter, shortening, and milk mixture into flour mixture; cover dough and refrigerate until firm, about 1 hour.

Step 4

Preheat oven to 350 degrees F (175 degrees C). Line baking sheets with parchment paper.

Step 5

Roll dough out on a lightly floured surface about 1/8-inch thick; cut dough circles with a round cookie cutter. Place about 1 tablespoon date mixture in the center of each circle; fold circle in half and press edges together tightly to seal. Place cookies on the prepared baking sheets.

Step 6

Bake in the preheated oven until golden, about 10 minutes. Remove to cool completely on a wire rack.

Nutrition Facts

Per Serving:

497.4 calories; protein 5.6g 11% DV; carbohydrates 81.5g 26% DV; fat 18.2g 28% DV; cholesterol 21.1mg 7% DV; sodium 174.9mg 7% DV.

Peanut Butter Temptations II

Servings: 18 **Yield:** 3 dozen

Ingredients

- ½ cup butter
- ½ cup white sugar
- ½ cup packed brown sugar
- ½ cup peanut butter
- 1 egg
- ½ teaspoon vanilla extract
- 1 ¼ cups all-purpose flour
- ¾ teaspoon baking soda
- ½ teaspoon salt
- 36 eaches miniature chocolate covered peanut butter cups, unwrapped

Directions

Step 1

Preheat oven to 375 degrees F (190 degrees C).

Step 2

In a medium bowl, cream together the brown sugar, white sugar and butter. Stir in the peanut butter, then the egg and vanilla. Sift together the flour, baking soda and salt, stir into the peanut butter mixture until the dough comes together. Shape into 1 inch balls and press them into the cups of an unprepared mini muffin pan.

Step 3

Bake for 8 to 10 minutes in the preheated oven. As soon as the cookies come out of the oven, press a mini chocolate covered peanut butter cup down into the center of each cookie until only the top is showing. Allow the cookies to cool completely before removing from their pans.

Nutrition Facts

Per Serving:

248.3 calories; protein 4.7g 9% DV; carbohydrates 28.3g 9% DV; fat 13.8g 21% DV; cholesterol 24.8mg 8% DV; sodium 241mg 10% DV.

German Lebkuchen

Prep: 15 mins **Cook:** 12 mins **Additional:** 7 hrs 53 mins **Total:** 8 hrs 20 mins **Servings:** 36 **Yield:** 3 dozen

Ingredients

- 1 egg
- ¾ cup brown sugar
- ½ cup honey
- ½ cup dark molasses
- 3 cups sifted all-purpose flour
- ½ teaspoon baking soda
- 1 ¼ teaspoons ground nutmeg
- 1 ¼ teaspoons ground cinnamon
- ½ teaspoon ground cloves

- ½ teaspoon ground allspice
- ½ cup slivered almonds
- ½ cup candied mixed fruit peel, finely chopped
- 1 egg white, beaten
- 1 tablespoon lemon juice
- ½ teaspoon lemon zest
- 1 ½ cups sifted confectioners' sugar

Directions

Step 1

In a large bowl, beat the egg, brown sugar and honey until smooth. Stir in the molasses. Combine the flour, baking soda, nutmeg, cinnamon, cloves and allspice; stir into the molasses mixture. Stir in the almonds and candied fruit peel. Cover or wrap dough, and chill overnight.

Step 2

Preheat the oven to 400 degrees F (200 degrees C). Grease cookie sheets. On a lightly floured surface, roll the dough out to 1/4 inch in thickness. Cut into 2x3 inch rectangles. Place cookies 1 1/2 inches apart onto cookie sheets.

Step 3

Bake for 10 to 12 minutes in the preheated oven, until firm. While still warm, brush the cookies with the lemon glaze.

Step 4

To make the glaze: In a small bowl, stir together the egg white, lemon juice and lemon zest. Mix in the confectioners' sugar until smooth. Brush over cookies.

Nutrition Facts

Per Serving:

119.9 calories; protein 1.7g 3% DV; carbohydrates 26.6g 9% DV; fat 1.1g 2% DV; cholesterol 5.2mg 2% DV; sodium 24.1mg 1% DV.

Peppermint Meringue Cookies

Prep: 15 mins **Cook:** 1 hr 30 mins **Total:** 1 hr 45 mins **Servings:** 56 **Yield:** 56 cookies

Ingredients

- 2 large egg whites egg whites
- ⅛ teaspoon cider vinegar
- ⅛ teaspoon salt
- ⅓ cup white sugar
- 3 eaches peppermint candy canes, crushed

Directions

Step 1

Preheat the oven to 225 degrees F (110 degrees C). Line cookie sheets with aluminum foil or parchment paper.

Step 2

In a large glass or metal bowl, whip egg whites, vinegar and salt to soft peaks. Gradually add sugar while continuing to whip until stiff peaks form, about 5 minutes. Fold in 1/3 of the crushed candy canes, reserving the rest. Drop by heaping teaspoonfuls, one inch apart onto the prepared cookie sheets. Sprinkle remaining crushed candy canes over the top.

Step 3

Bake for 90 minutes in the preheated oven, or until dry. Cool on baking sheets.

Nutrition Facts

Per Serving:

11.1 calories; protein 0.1g; carbohydrates 2.7g 1% DV; fatg; cholesterolmg; sodium 7.7mg.

Pebber Nodder (Danish Christmas Cookies)

Prep: 15 mins **Cook:** 10 mins **Total:** 25 mins **Servings:** 100 **Yield:** 100 cookies

Ingredients

- 1 cup butter
- 1 cup sugar
- 2 large eggs eggs
- 2 ½ cups all-purpose flour
- 1 teaspoon ground cardamom
- 1 teaspoon ground cinnamon, or to taste

Directions

Step 1

Preheat the oven to 350 degrees F (175 degrees C).

Step 2

In a large bowl, mix together the butter and sugar until smooth. Beat in the eggs one at a time, stirring until light and fluffy. Combine the flour, cardamom and cinnamon; stir into the sugar mixture just until blended.

Step 3

Separate the dough into 6 balls, and roll each ball into a rope about as big around as your finger on a lightly floured surface. Cut into 1/2-inch pieces, and place them on an ungreased baking sheet.

Step 4

Bake for 10 minutes in the preheated oven, or until lightly browned. Cool on baking sheets for a few minutes, then transfer to wire racks to cool completely.

Nutrition Facts

Per Serving:

36.9 calories; protein 0.5g 1% DV; carbohydrates 4.4g 1% DV; fat 2g 3% DV; cholesterol 8.6mg 3% DV; sodium 14.5mg 1% DV.

Mandelmakronen (Almond Meringues)

Prep: 20 mins **Cook:** 15 mins **Total:** 35 mins **Servings:** 48 **Yield:** 48 cookies

Ingredients

- 4 large egg whites egg whites
- 1 cup white sugar
- 1 ½ cups almond flour, or more as needed
- ¼ teaspoon ground cinnamon

Directions

Step 1

Preheat oven to 300 degrees F (150 degrees C). Line 2 baking sheets with parchment paper.

Step 2

Beat egg whites in a glass, metal, or ceramic bowl until stiff peaks form. Gradually add sugar, 1 teaspoon at a time, while continuing to beat at high speed. Combine ground almonds and cinnamon in a bowl and fold into the egg white mixture with a spatula. Add more ground almonds if mixture is too runny.

Step 3

Use 2 teaspoons to place little mounds of almond mixture 2 inches apart onto the prepared baking sheets.

Step 4

Bake in the preheated oven until lightly browned and baked through, 15 to 20 minutes. Carefully remove from baking sheets and cool on wire racks.

Nutrition Facts

Per Serving:

40.2 calories; protein 1.1g 2% DV; carbohydrates 5g 2% DV; fat 1.9g 3% DV; cholesterolmg; sodium 4.6mg.

German Walnut Shortbread Cookies

Prep: 20 mins **Cook:** 15 mins **Additional:** 1 hr 20 mins **Total:** 1 hr 55 mins **Servings:** 80 **Yield:** 80 cookies

Ingredients

- ¾ cup unsalted butter, at room temperature
- 2 tablespoons unsalted butter, room temperature
- ¾ cup confectioners' sugar
- 4 teaspoons confectioners' sugar
- 1 egg yolk
- 1 pinch salt
- 2 ¼ cups all-purpose flour
- 2 tablespoons all-purpose flour
- ¾ cup chopped walnuts
- 2 tablespoons chopped walnuts

Directions

Step 1

Beat 3/4 cup plus 2 tablespoons butter in a large bowl using an electric mixer until creamy. Add 3/4 cup plus 4 teaspoons confectioner's sugar, egg yolk, and salt; beat until smooth. Knead in 2 1/4 cups plus 2 tablespoons flour and 3/4 cup plus 2 tablespoons walnuts.

Step 2

Shape dough into 2-inch thick rolls and press them into rectangles using a flat item like a cutting board (they should look like oversized butter sticks). Wrap in plastic wrap and refrigerate until firm, about 1 hour.

Step 3

Preheat oven to 375 degrees F (190 degrees C).

Step 4

Cut dough into thin slices and lay them on an ungreased baking sheet.

Step 5

Bake in the preheated oven for 10 minutes. Reduce heat to 250 degrees F (120 degrees C) and bake until very lightly browned, about 5 more minutes.

Step 6

Remove from the baking sheet and cool on a wire rack, about 20 minutes.

Nutrition Facts

Per Serving:

45.4 calories; protein 0.6g 1% DV; carbohydrates 4.3g 1% DV; fat 3g 5% DV; cholesterol 7.9mg 3% DV; sodium 4.4mg.

Linzer Torte Cookies

Servings: 15 Yield: 30 cookies

Ingredients

- ¾ cup butter, softened
- 1 cup white sugar
- 1 egg
- 1 teaspoon lemon zest
- 2 cups all-purpose flour
- ¾ cup blanched slivered almonds, ground
- 1 teaspoon ground cinnamon
- ⅛ teaspoon ground cloves
- 1 cup raspberry jam

Directions

Step 1

Preheat oven to 350 degrees F (175 degrees C). Grease an 11x7 inch baking pan.

Step 2

In a medium bowl, cream together the butter and sugar. Beat in the egg and lemon peel. In another bowl, stir together the flour, almonds, cinnamon and cloves. Gradually stir the dry ingredients into the creamed mixture. The dough will be stiff, so you may need to knead it by hand to get it to come together. Press half of the dough into the bottom of the prepared pan.

Step 3

Press half of the dough into the bottom of the prepared pan. Spread the preserves over the crust. On a lightly floured surface, roll the remaining dough into long rope about 1/2 inch in diameter. Place lengths of the rope across the top of the jam in a lattice pattern over the preserves.

Step 4

Bake 40 minutes or until top is golden. Cool in pan on wire rack. Cut into 2 inch by 1 inch bars.

Nutrition Facts

Per Serving:

288.2 calories; protein 3.4g 7% DV; carbohydrates 42g 14% DV; fat 12.5g 19% DV; cholesterol 36.8mg 12% DV; sodium 71mg 3% DV.

Easy Vegan Gingerbread Cookies

Prep: 10 mins **Cook:** 8 mins **Additional:** 2 hrs **Total:** 2 hrs 18 mins **Servings:** 24 **Yield:** 24 cookies

Ingredients

- 1 ½ cups all-purpose flour
- 1 teaspoon baking powder
- 1 teaspoon ground cinnamon
- ½ teaspoon baking soda
- ½ teaspoon ground ginger
- ½ teaspoon ground allspice

- ¼ teaspoon salt
- ½ cup coconut oil, at room temperature
- ⅓ cup molasses
- ¼ cup white sugar
- 1 teaspoon vanilla extract

Directions

Step 1

Preheat oven to 350 degrees F (175 degrees C). Line 2 baking sheets with parchment paper.

Step 2

Sift flour, baking powder, cinnamon, baking soda, ginger, allspice, and salt into a bowl.

Step 3

Cream coconut oil, molasses, and sugar in a bowl with an electric mixer; add vanilla extract. Stir in flour mixture; mix until a sticky dough forms, about 2 minutes. Wrap dough in plastic wrap and chill for 2 hours.

Step 4

Roll out dough on a floured surface to 1/4 to 1/2-inch thickness. Dip cookie cutter in flour, cut out cookies, and place on the prepared baking sheets.

Step 5

Bake in the preheated oven until lightly golden, 8 to 10 minutes.

Nutrition Facts

Per Serving:

90 calories; protein 0.8g 2% DV; carbohydrates 11.7g 4% DV; fat 4.6g 7% DV; cholesterolmg; sodium 72.7mg 3% DV.

Classic Butter Cookies II

Servings: 48 **Yield:** 3 to 4 dozen

Ingredients

- 2 ½ cups all-purpose flour
- 1 cup butter
- ½ cup white sugar
- 1 egg
- ½ teaspoon almond extract

Directions

Step 1

Cream the butter until light. Gradually add the sugar and beat until light and fluffy. Beat in the egg and almond extract.

Step 2

Gradually blend in the flour. Cover and chill dough for at least 1 hour.

Step 3

Preheat oven to 350 degrees F (175 degrees C).

Step 4

Roll dough out on a lightly floured surface to 1/8 inch thickness. Cut into desired shapes, using lightly floured cookie cutters. Place cookies on ungreased cookie sheets.

Step 5

Bake at 350 degrees F (175 degrees C) for 8 to 12 minutes or until golden. Remove to wire racks to cool completely. Decorate as desired.

Nutrition Facts

Per Serving:

67.3 calories; protein 0.8g 2% DV; carbohydrates 7.1g 2% DV; fat 4g 6% DV; cholesterol 14mg 5% DV; sodium 28.8mg 1% DV.

Crazy Yummy Cranberry Pecan Cookies with Orange Glaze

Prep: 25 mins **Cook:** 10 mins **Additional:** 15 mins **Total:** 50 mins **Servings:** 48 **Yield:** 4 dozen cookies

Ingredients

Cookie:

- 2 ¼ cups all-purpose flour
- 1 teaspoon baking soda
- 1 teaspoon salt
- 1 cup butter
- ¾ cup white sugar
- ¾ cup brown sugar, packed
- 1 teaspoon vanilla extract
- 2 large eggs eggs

- 1 cup chopped pecans
- 1 cup rolled oats

Glaze:

- 1 ½ cups confectioners' sugar
- ½ cup freshly squeezed orange juice
- 1 orange, zested
- 1 tablespoon butter

- 1 cup sweetened dried cranberries (such as Ocean Spray Craisins)

Directions

Step 1

Preheat an oven to 375 degrees F (190 degrees C). Sift the flour, baking soda, and salt together in a bowl.

Step 2

In a large bowl, beat together the butter, white and brown sugars, and vanilla extract with an electric mixer until the mixture is creamy and well blended. Beat in eggs, one at a time, and then gradually beat in the flour just until the mixture makes a soft dough. Stir in the pecans, rolled oats, and cranberries, and drop by heaping spoonfuls onto ungreased baking sheets.

Step 3

Bake in the preheated oven until the cookies are set and the edges are slightly brown, 10 to 12 minutes. Let the cookies cool for 1 minute on baking sheets before removing to wire racks to finish cooling. Glaze cookies while still a little warm.

Step 4

Place the confectioners' sugar and orange juice in a microwave-safe bowl, and stir to dissolve the sugar. Stir in the orange zest and butter, and microwave on medium power until the butter melts and the mixture is warm, about 30 seconds. Stir the warm glaze until smooth, and drizzle over cookies.

Nutrition Facts

Per Serving:

131.2 calories; protein 1.4g 3% DV; carbohydrates 18.6g 6% DV; fat 6.1g 9% DV; cholesterol 18.6mg 6% DV; sodium 107.8mg 4% DV.

Czechoslovakian Cookies

Servings: 12 **Yield:** 2 dozen

Ingredients

- 1 cup butter
- 1 cup white sugar
- 2 large egg yolks egg yolks
- 1 teaspoon vanilla extract
- ⅛ teaspoon ground cardamom
- ¼ teaspoon ground allspice
- 2 cups all-purpose flour
- 1 cup chopped pecans
- ½ cup strawberry jam

Directions

Step 1

Preheat oven to 325 degrees F (165 degrees C). Grease one 8 inch square baking dish.

Step 2

Cream the butter until soft and fluffy. Add the white sugar gradually, until light and fluffy. Beat in the egg yolks.

Step 3

Sift the cardamom, allspice and flour together. Gradually add it to the butter mixture and stir to combine well. Stir in the chopped pecans.

Step 4

Spoon 1/2 of the dough into the prepared pan, spreading evenly. Top with strawberry jam and cover with the remaining dough.

Step 5

Bake at 325 degrees F (165 degrees C) for 1 hour or until lightly browned. Cool then cut into 1 1/2 inch sized squares.

Nutrition Facts

Per Serving:

384.1 calories; protein 3.6g 7% DV; carbohydrates 43.2g 14% DV; fat 22.8g 35% DV; cholesterol 74.8mg 25% DV; sodium 110.8mg 4% DV.

Chinese Christmas Cookies

Prep: 15 mins **Additional:** 2 hrs **Total:** 2 hrs 15 mins **Servings:** 24 **Yield:** 24 cookies

Ingredients

- 1 cup semisweet chocolate chips
- 1 cup peanut butter chips

- 1 cup chow mein noodles
- 1 cup dry-roasted peanuts

Directions

Step 1

Melt chocolate and peanut butter chips in the top of a double boiler over simmering water, stirring frequently, until smooth.

Step 2

Mix chow mein noodles and peanuts in a large mixing bowl. Pour chocolate mixture over noodles and peanuts and turn to coat.

Step 3

Line a baking sheet with waxed paper. Drop mixture by rounded tablespoonfuls onto prepared sheet. Refrigerate until set, about 2 hours.

Nutrition Facts

Per Serving:

135.7 calories; protein 4g 8% DV; carbohydrates 11.8g 4% DV; fat 8.5g 13% DV; cholesterolmg; sodium 83.3mg 3% DV.

Cheesecake Topped Brownies

Prep: 20 mins **Cook:** 45 mins **Total:** 1 hr 5 mins **Servings:** 40 **Yield:** 1 - 9x13 inch pan

Ingredients

- 1 (21.5 ounce) package brownie mix
- 1 (8 ounce) package cream cheese, softened
- 2 tablespoons butter, softened
- 1 tablespoon cornstarch
- 1 (14 ounce) can sweetened condensed milk
- 1 egg
- 1 teaspoon vanilla extract
- 1 (16 ounce) container prepared chocolate frosting

Directions

Step 1

Preheat oven 350 degrees F (175 degrees C). Grease a 9x13 inch baking pan.

Step 2

Prepare brownie mix according to the directions on the package. Spread into prepared baking pan.

Step 3

In a medium bowl, beat cream cheese, butter and cornstarch until fluffy. Gradually beat in sweetened condensed milk, egg and vanilla until smooth. Pour cream cheese mixture evenly over brownie batter.

Step 4

Bake in preheated oven for 45 minutes, or until top is lightly browned. Allow to cool, spread with frosting, and cut into bars. Store covered in refrigerator, or freeze in a single layer for up to 2 weeks.

Nutrition Facts

Per Serving:

169.6 calories; protein 2.1g 4% DV; carbohydrates 24.4g 8% DV; fat 7.7g 12% DV; cholesterol 15.7mg 5% DV; sodium 101.6mg 4% DV.

Chocolate Cantucci

Prep: 20 mins **Cook:** 15 mins **Additional:** 45 mins **Total:** 1 hr 20 mins **Servings:** 20 **Yield:** 20 cantucci

Ingredients

- 1 ¼ cups white sugar
- 3 eaches eggs
- 1 teaspoon vanilla extract

- 2 ½ cups all-purpose flour
- 2 teaspoons baking powder
- ¾ cup chopped dark chocolate

Directions

Step 1

Preheat oven to 350 degrees F (175 degrees C). Line a baking sheet with parchment paper.

Step 2

Combine sugar, eggs, and vanilla extract in a large bowl; beat with an electric mixer until frothy. Add flour and baking powder and mix well. Fold in chocolate pieces until a sticky dough forms. Separate dough into 2 portions and shape each portion into a long, thick log. Place logs 2 inches apart on the prepared baking sheet.

Step 3

Bake logs in the preheated oven until golden brown, 15 to 20 minutes.

Step 4

Remove logs from the oven and cool until easily handled, about 5 minutes. Transfer to a cutting board; slice logs diagonally into 3/4-inch slices using a serrated knife.

Step 5

Return cantucci slices to the baking sheet and return to the oven. Turn off oven and allow cantucci to dry in the warm oven for 30 minutes. Cool to room temperature, about 10 minutes, before serving.

Nutrition Facts

Per Serving:

145.9 calories; protein 2.8g 6% DV; carbohydrates 28.9g 9% DV; fat 2.5g 4% DV; cholesterol 24.6mg 8% DV; sodium 60mg 2% DV.

Cinnamon Stars

Servings: 18 **Yield:** 3 dozen

Ingredients

- 2 ⅔ cups finely ground almonds
- 1 tablespoon ground cinnamon
- 1 teaspoon lemon zest
- ⅓ cup egg whites
- ⅛ teaspoon salt
- 2 ½ cups confectioners' sugar
- 1 ¾ teaspoons lemon juice

Directions

Step 1

Stir together the almonds, cinnamon, and lemon zest until combined.

Step 2

Beat the egg whites and salt until soft peaks form. Slowly sift in the confectioner's sugar, continuing to beat until the mixture is stiff. Set aside 1/3 cup of the egg white mixture for the glaze. Fold in the almond mixture.

Step 3

Preheat oven to 325 degrees F (170 degrees C). Line the cookie sheets with parchment paper.

Step 4

Roll the dough to 1/4 inch thickness on a surface that has been sprinkled with confectioners' sugar. Using a 2 1/2-inch star cookie cutter, cut out the cookies and place them on the cookie sheets.

Step 5

To make the glaze, add the lemon juice to the reserved egg white mixture, stirring until smooth. Brush the tops of the cookies lightly with the glaze. (If the glaze starts to thicken, add a few more drops of lemon juice.)

Step 6

Bake for 20 to 25 minutes. When done, they will be light brown and soft in the center. Remove and cool on wire racks.

Nutrition Facts

Per Serving:

189.7 calories; protein 5g 10% DV; carbohydrates 21.2g 7% DV; fat 10.7g 16% DV; cholesterolmg; sodium 24mg 1% DV.

Chocolate Pecan Pie Bars

Prep: 20 mins **Cook:** 40 mins **Additional:** 30 mins **Total:** 1 hr 30 mins **Servings:** 40 **Yield:** 40 bars

Ingredients

Crust:

- 2 cups all-purpose flour
- ⅓ cup white sugar
- ⅓ teaspoon salt
- ⅔ cup margarine

Filling:

- 1 ½ cups light corn syrup (such as Karo)
- 1 cup brown sugar
- 4 large eggs eggs
- 3 tablespoons margarine
- 1 ½ teaspoons vanilla extract
- ⅛ teaspoon salt
- 1 ½ cups chopped pecans
- 1 (11 ounce) package chocolate chips

Directions

Step 1

Preheat the oven to 350 degrees F (175 degrees C). Lightly grease a 10x15-inch jelly roll pan.

Step 2

Stir flour, white sugar, and salt together in a large bowl. Cut in 2/3 cup margarine until mixture resembles coarse crumbs. Press mixture into the bottom of the prepared pan.

Step 3

Bake in the preheated oven for 20 minutes.

Step 4

While the crust is baking, prepare the filling by mixing corn syrup, brown sugar, eggs, margarine, vanilla extract, and salt together in a large bowl until smooth. Stir in pecans.

Step 5

Remove the crust from the oven and sprinkle with chocolate chips. Spread filling evenly over the chocolate chip covered crust.

Step 6

Bake in the preheated oven until set, 20 to 25 minutes. Cool completely before cutting into squares.

Nutrition Facts

Per Serving:

194.1 calories; protein 2.1g 4% DV; carbohydrates 26.9g 9% DV; fat 9.9g 15% DV; cholesterol 18.6mg 6% DV; sodium 88.2mg 4% DV.

Red Velvet Chocolate Chip Cookies

Prep: 20 mins **Cook:** 10 mins **Additional:** 1 hr **Total:** 1 hr 30 mins **Servings:** 15 **Yield:** 15 cookies

Ingredients

- 1 ½ cups all-purpose flour
- ⅓ cup unsweetened cocoa powder
- 1 teaspoon baking soda
- ½ teaspoon baking powder
- ½ teaspoon salt

- ½ cup butter, softened
- ¾ cup brown sugar
- ¼ cup white sugar
- 1 egg
- 1 ½ tablespoons milk

- 1 ½ teaspoons vanilla extract
- 2 tablespoons red food coloring
- 1 cup dark chocolate chips, or as needed

Directions

Step 1

Whisk flour, cocoa powder, baking soda, baking powder, and salt together in a bowl.

Step 2

Beat butter with an electric mixer until fluffy, about 2 minutes; beat in brown sugar and white sugar until smooth, about 1 minute. Beat egg, milk, and vanilla extract into butter mixture; beat in food coloring until uniformly colored.

Step 3

Stir flour mixture into butter mixture gradually with electric mixer on low speed until combined; stir in 1 cup chocolate chips. Cover bowl with plastic wrap; place in the refrigerator for 1 hour or up to overnight.

Step 4

Preheat oven to 350 degrees F (175 degrees C). Line baking sheets with parchment paper.

Step 5

Roll dough into 2-inch balls; place on prepared baking sheets and flatten slightly.

Step 6

Bake in the preheated oven until edges are lightly browned, about 10 minutes. Sprinkle cookies with a few additional chocolate chips; allow to cool completely.

Nutrition Facts

Per Serving:

205.3 calories; protein 2.8g 6% DV; carbohydrates 28.9g 9% DV; fat 9.9g 15% DV; cholesterol 28.8mg 10% DV; sodium 232.3mg 9% DV.

Gluten-Free Gingersnap Cookies

Prep: 15 mins **Cook:** 10 mins **Additional:** 1 hr 5 mins **Total:** 1 hr 30 mins **Servings:** 25 **Yield:** 25 cookies

Ingredients

- ¾ cup unsalted butter, softened
- ½ cup brown sugar

- ½ cup unbleached cane sugar
- 1 egg
- ¼ cup blackstrap molasses
- 1 teaspoon vanilla extract
- 1 cup oat flour
- ½ cup almond flour
- ⅓ cup coconut flour
- 1 (1/4 inch thick) slice fresh ginger, grated
- 1 tablespoon ground ginger
- 1 teaspoon baking soda
- 1 teaspoon ground cinnamon
- 1 teaspoon ground nutmeg
- ½ teaspoon ground cloves
- ¼ cup unbleached cane sugar, or as needed
- ½ teaspoon ground cinnamon, or as needed
- ¼ teaspoon ground nutmeg, or as needed

Directions

Step 1

Beat butter, brown sugar, and 1/2 cup cane sugar together in a bowl using an electric mixer until creamy. Add egg and mix to combine. Mix in molasses and vanilla extract.

Step 2

Mix oat flour, almond flour, coconut flour, fresh ginger, ground ginger, baking soda, 1 teaspoon cinnamon, 1 teaspoon nutmeg, and cloves together in a separate bowl. Add to butter mixture slowly and combine. Refrigerate dough for at least 1 hour, to overnight; dough will be very wet before it's chilled.

Step 3

Preheat the oven to 350 degrees F (175 degrees C). Line 2 large baking sheets with parchment paper.

Step 4

Combine 1/4 cup cane sugar, 1/2 teaspoon cinnamon, and 1/4 teaspoon nutmeg in a shallow dish.

Step 5

Scoop dough by tablespoonfuls and roll into balls. Roll balls in cinnamon-sugar mixture to coat and place onto the prepared baking sheets, making sure not to overcrowd as they will flatten and spread.

Step 6

Bake in the preheated oven until set and golden, 10 to 12 minutes. Let cookies sit for 5 minutes before transferring to a wire rack to cool. Serve warm or let cool completely before storing in an airtight container.

Nutrition Facts

Per Serving:

123.2 calories; protein 1.6g 3% DV; carbohydrates 13g 4% DV; fat 7.6g 12% DV; cholesterol 22.1mg 7% DV; sodium 57.2mg 2% DV.

Children's Gingerbread House

Servings: 15 **Yield:** 1 gingerbread house

Ingredients

- ¾ cup butter
- ⅞ cup packed light brown sugar
- 1 teaspoon lemon zest
- 1 ½ tablespoons lemon juice
- ½ cup molasses
- 2 large eggs eggs
- 3 cups all-purpose flour

- 2 teaspoons baking powder
- 1 tablespoon ground ginger
- 2 teaspoons ground allspice
- 6 large egg whites egg whites
- 4 (16 ounce) packages confectioners' sugar, sifted

Directions

Step 1

First cut out in thin cardboard: a side wall, 4 1/2 x 8 inches; an end wall, 4 1/2x5 inches; a triangular gable, 4 1/2x3x3 inches; and a roof rectangle, 4 1/2x9 inches. Tape the rectangular end wall piece to the triangular gable piece: match the long side of the triangle, 4 1/2 inches, to one of the 4 1/2 inch sides of the end wall.

Step 2

In a large bowl, cream butter and sugar until light and fluffy. Stir in lemon zest, lemon juice, and molasses. Gradually beat in 2 eggs. Sift the flour, baking powder, and spices together; stir into creamed mixture. Wrap dough in parchment paper, and refrigerate for 1 hour.

Step 3

Turn out dough onto a lightly floured surface. Divide into 6 portions, 2 slightly larger than the others. On a lightly floured surface, roll out the 4 smaller pieces to approximately the size of the side wall and the end wall with gable templates; cut out two of each. Roll out remaining dough, and cut into two rectangular roof pieces. Transfer gingerbread onto greased baking trays.

Step 4

In a preheated 375 degree F (190 degrees C) oven, bake gingerbread for 10 minutes, or until crisp. When removing from the oven, leave the gingerbread on the baking trays for a few minutes to set, then transfer to wire racks. Leave out overnight to harden.

Step 5

In a large bowl, lightly whisk 2 egg whites. Gradually beat in approximately 5 cups confectioners' sugar. The icing should be smooth and stand in firm peaks. Spread or pipe a 9 inch line of icing onto a cake board, and press in one of the side walls so that it sticks firmly and stands upright. If necessary, spread or pipe a little extra icing along either side to help support it. Take an end wall and ice both the side edges. Spread or pipe a line of icing on the board at a right angle to the first wall, and press the end wall into position. Repeat this process with the other two walls until they are all in position. Leave the walls to harden together for at least two hours before putting on the roof. Spread or pipe a thick layer of icing on top of all the walls, and fix the roof pieces in position; the roof should overlap the walls to make the eaves. Pipe or spread a little icing along the crest of the roof to hold the two pieces firmly together. Leave overnight to set firmly.

Step 6

When ready to decorate, make the remaining icing. In a large bowl, lightly whisk 4 egg whites, and mix in remaining confectioners' sugar as before. Use this to make snow on the roof, and to stick various candies for decoration. Finish with a fine dusting of sifted confectioners' sugar.

Nutrition Facts

Per Serving:

736.2 calories; protein 5g 10% DV; carbohydrates 159.7g 52% DV; fat 10.3g 16% DV; cholesterol 49.2mg 16% DV; sodium 171.6mg 7% DV.

Icelandic Pepper Cookies

Servings: 18 **Yield:** 3 dozen

Ingredients

- 1 ¼ cups butter, softened
- 1 ¼ cups white sugar
- ¾ cup light corn syrup
- 2 small eggs
- 3 cups all-purpose flour
- 1 ½ teaspoons baking powder
- 1 teaspoon baking soda
- ½ teaspoon salt
- 2 teaspoons ground cinnamon
- 2 teaspoons ground cloves
- 1 teaspoon ground ginger
- ¼ teaspoon ground black pepper

Directions

Step 1

In a large bowl, cream butter and sugar. Stir in corn syrup and eggs; cream well. Sift together flour, baking powder, baking soda, salt, cinnamon, cloves, ginger, and pepper. Add dry ingredients to the butter mixture, and mix until smooth. Refrigerate dough over night.

Step 2

Preheat oven to 350 degrees F (175 degrees C).

Step 3

Roll out dough to 1/4 inch thickness. Cut out cookies with a 2 inch round cookie cutter. Place at least 1 inch apart on cookie sheet and bake for 8 to 10 minutes in preheated oven.

Nutrition Facts

Per Serving:

289.2 calories; protein 2.8g 6% DV; carbohydrates 40.9g 13% DV; fat 13.5g 21% DV; cholesterol 49.2mg 16% DV; sodium 281.2mg 11% DV.

Raisin Butter Tart Squares

Prep: 20 mins **Cook:** 35 mins **Additional:** 35 mins **Total:** 1 hr 30 mins **Servings:** 16 **Yield:** 1 9x9-inch pan

Ingredients

- 1 cup raisins
- 1 cup hot water, or as needed

Crust:

- 1 ½ cups all-purpose flour
- ½ cup butter, softened
- ¼ cup packed brown sugar

Filling:

- 1 cup brown sugar
- ⅓ cup butter, softened
- 1 egg
- 1 teaspoon vanilla extract
- 1 teaspoon heavy whipping cream
- 1 tablespoon all-purpose flour

Directions

Step 1

Preheat oven to 325 degrees F (165 degrees C).

Step 2

Place raisins in a cup; pour in hot water to cover, and set aside to soak, about 5 minutes.

Step 3

Place 1 1/2 cups flour in a large bowl; cut in 1/2 cup butter until crumbly. Stir 1/4 cup brown sugar into flour mixture; press mixture evenly into the bottom of a 9x9-inch pan.

Step 4

Bake in the preheated oven until lightly browned, about 15 minutes. Remove from oven, leaving oven on.

Step 5

Beat 1 cup brown sugar and 1/3 cup butter together until smooth; stir in egg, vanilla extract, and cream. Strain raisins; stir raisins and 1 tablespoon flour into butter mixture. Pour raisin mixture over crust.

Step 6

Bake in the preheated oven until filling is bubbly, about 20 minutes. Allow to cool before cutting into squares, about 30 minutes.

Nutrition Facts

Per Serving:

227.9 calories; protein 2.1g 4% DV; carbohydrates 33.4g 11% DV; fat 10.2g 16% DV; cholesterol 37.5mg 13% DV; sodium 79.1mg 3% DV.

Norwegian Butter Cookies

Servings: 12 **Yield:** 1 dozen

Ingredients

- ½ cup butter

- 2 large eggs eggs
- ¼ cup white sugar
- 1 cup all-purpose flour
- ½ teaspoon vanilla extract

Directions

Step 1

Preheat oven to 375 degrees F (190 degrees C).

Step 2

Hard boil the eggs and separate the yolks. Cream the butter and hard boiled egg yolks. Beat in the sugar and add the flour vanilla extract. Mix thoroughly. Put through a cookie press or arrange by teaspoonfuls on ungreased cookie sheets.

Step 3

Bake 10 to 12 minutes, or until lightly browned.

Nutrition Facts

Per Serving:

134.3 calories; protein 2.2g 4% DV; carbohydrates 12.2g 4% DV; fat 8.6g 13% DV; cholesterol 51.3mg 17% DV; sodium 66.4mg 3% DV.

Eggnog Thumbprints

Prep: 20 mins **Cook:** 12 mins **Additional:** 28 mins **Total:** 1 hr **Servings:** 48 **Yield:** 4 dozen

Ingredients

- ¾ cup butter, softened
- ½ cup white sugar
- ¼ cup packed brown sugar
- 1 egg
- ½ teaspoon vanilla extract
- 2 cups all-purpose flour
- ¼ teaspoon salt
- ¼ cup butter
- 1 cup confectioners' sugar
- 1 tablespoon rum
- 1 pinch ground nutmeg

Directions

Step 1

Preheat the oven to 350 degrees F (175 degrees C).

Step 2

In a medium bowl, cream together 3/4 cup butter, white sugar, and brown sugar until smooth. Beat in egg and vanilla. Combine flour and salt; stir into the creamed mixture by hand to form a soft dough. Roll dough into 1 inch balls, and place balls 2 inches apart on ungreased cookie sheets. Make an indention in the center of each cookie using your finger or thumb.

Step 3

Bake for 12 minutes in preheated oven. Cool completely.

Step 4

In a small bowl, mix together 1/4 cup butter, confectioners' sugar, and rum. Spoon rounded teaspoonfuls of filling onto cookies. Sprinkle with nutmeg. Let stand until set before storing in an airtight container.

Nutrition Facts

Per Serving:

77.4 calories; protein 0.7g 1% DV; carbohydrates 9.7g 3% DV; fat 4g 6% DV; cholesterol 14mg 5% DV; sodium 41.3mg 2% DV.

Storybook Gingerbread Men

Servings: 5 Yield: 10 cookies

Ingredients

- ½ cup shortening
- ½ cup packed brown sugar
- 3 ¼ cups sifted all-purpose flour
- 1 teaspoon salt
- 1 teaspoon baking soda
- ½ teaspoon ground cinnamon
- ½ teaspoon ground ginger
- ¾ cup molasses
- ¼ cup water

Directions

Step 1

Cream shortening and sugar. Sift flour with salt, soda and spices. Blend flour mixture into creamed mixture alternately with molasses and water. Chill at least 1 hour.

Step 2

Preheat oven to 350 degrees F (180 degrees C).

Step 3

Roll dough to 1/4 inch thick. Cut with large 6-8 inch gingerbread men cookie cutters. Lift onto lightly greased cookie sheet with broad spatula.

Step 4

Bake above oven center for about 12 minutes or until cookies spring back lightly in center. Do not overcook, they won't stay soft. Remove from sheets. Cool on wire racks. Makes 10 men 6-8 inches tall.

Nutrition Facts

Per Serving:

704.4 calories; protein 8.4g 17% DV; carbohydrates 120.7g 39% DV; fat 21.4g 33% DV; cholesterolmg; sodium 743.2mg 30% DV.

No-Bake Chocolate Peanut Butter Bars

Prep: 15 mins **Additional:** 1 hr **Total:** 1 hr 15 mins **Servings:** 60 **Yield:** 60 servings

Ingredients

- 2 cups peanut butter, divided
- ¾ cup butter, softened
- 2 cups powdered sugar
- 3 cups graham cracker crumbs
- 1 (12 ounce) package NESTLE TOLL HOUSE Semi-Sweet Chocolate Mini Morsels, divided

Directions

Step 1

Grease 13 x 9-inch baking pan.

Step 2

Beat 1 1/4 cups peanut butter and butter in large mixer bowl until creamy. Gradually beat in 1 cup powdered sugar. With hands or wooden spoon, work in remaining powdered sugar, graham cracker crumbs and 1/2 cup morsels. Press evenly into prepared baking pan. Smooth top with spatula.

Step 3

Melt remaining peanut butter and remaining morsels in medium, heavy-duty saucepan over lowest possible heat, stirring constantly, until smooth. Spread over graham cracker crust in pan. Refrigerate for at least 1 hour or until chocolate is firm; cut into bars. Store in refrigerator.

Nutrition Facts

Per Serving:

134.8 calories; protein 2.8g 6% DV; carbohydrates 12.4g 4% DV; fat 8.9g 14% DV; cholesterol 8mg 3% DV; sodium 90.6mg 4% DV.

Mom's Nut Horns

Prep: 30 mins **Cook:** 20 mins **Additional:** 8 hrs **Total:** 8 hrs 50 mins **Servings:** 24 **Yield:** 48 small cookies

Ingredients

Dough:

- ½ pound butter
- 2 cups all-purpose flour
- ¾ cup sour cream
- 1 egg yolk

Filling:

- ¾ cup finely ground walnuts
- ¾ cup white sugar
- 1 teaspoon ground cinnamon

Directions

Step 1

Cut butter into flour in a bowl using 2 knives or a pastry blender until the mixture resembles coarse crumbs. Add sour cream and egg yolk; mix well. Shape the dough into a ball. Wrap in plastic wrap and refrigerate, 8 hours to overnight.

Step 2

Combine walnuts, sugar, and cinnamon in a small bowl.

Step 3

Preheat oven to 350 degrees F (175 degrees C). Lightly grease 2 baking sheets.

Step 4

Cut dough into 4 equal pieces. Roll each piece into a 1/8-inch thick circle on a lightly floured surface. Spread 1/4 of the walnut mixture on each circle; cut each circle into 12 wedge-shaped pieces with a pizza wheel.

Step 5

Shape each piece of dough into a crescent by rolling dough from the wide end of the wedge into the center. Transfer cookies carefully to the baking sheets.

Step 6

Bake in the preheated oven until golden, 20 to 25 minutes. Watch cookies carefully as they bake; their bottoms tend to brown faster than their tops.

Nutrition Facts

Per Serving:

171.6 calories; protein 2.1g 4% DV; carbohydrates 15.1g 5% DV; fat 11.8g 18% DV; cholesterol 32mg 11% DV; sodium 58.9mg 2% DV.

Spritz Cookies II

Servings: 24 **Yield:** 4 dozen

Ingredients

- 1 cup butter, softened
- 3 large egg yolks egg yolks
- 2 ½ cups all-purpose flour
- ⅔ cup white sugar
- 1 teaspoon vanilla extract

Directions

Step 1

Mix the butter or margarine, sugar, egg yolks and vanilla. Add the flour and mix by hand.

Step 2

Spoon into cookie press and press onto ungreased cookie sheets. Sprinkle with colored sugars.

Step 3

Bake in preheated 400 degrees F (200 degrees C) oven for 7-10 minutes.

Nutrition Facts

Per Serving:

143.8 calories; protein 1.8g 4% DV; carbohydrates 15.6g 5% DV; fat 8.4g 13% DV; cholesterol 45.9mg 15% DV; sodium 55.8mg 2% DV.

Gingerbread Cookies

Servings: 30 **Yield:** 2 1/2 dozen

Ingredients

- 1 ½ cups dark molasses
- 1 cup packed brown sugar
- ⅔ cup cold water
- ⅓ cup shortening
- 7 cups all-purpose flour
- 2 teaspoons baking soda
- 1 teaspoon salt
- 1 teaspoon ground allspice
- 2 teaspoons ground ginger
- 1 teaspoon ground cloves
- 1 teaspoon ground cinnamon
- 1 (16 ounce) package chocolate frosting

Directions

Step 1

Preheat the oven to 350 degrees F (175 degrees C). Lightly grease one cookie sheet.

Step 2

Mix together the molasses, brown sugar, water and shortening.

Step 3

Sift together the flour, baking soda, salt, allspice, ginger, cloves and cinnamon. Add to sugar mixture and mix well. Cover and refrigerate for 2 hours.

Step 4

Roll dough 1/4 inch thick on floured board. Cut with floured gingerbread cutter. Place about 2 inches apart on cookie sheet. Bake for 10-12 minutes. Cool and decorate with frosting.

Nutrition Facts

Per Serving:

263.9 calories; protein 3.2g 6% DV; carbohydrates 51.7g 17% DV; fat 5.3g 8% DV; cholesterolmg; sodium 198.7mg 8% DV.

Granny's Shortbread Cookies

Servings: 12 **Yield:** 2 dozen

Ingredients

- 1 cup butter, softened
- ½ cup confectioners' sugar
- ½ teaspoon salt
- ⅛ teaspoon ground nutmeg
- 1 egg yolk

- 2 cups all-purpose flour
- 1 (2.25 ounce) jar red decorator sugar
- 1 (10 ounce) jar maraschino cherries, drained

Directions

Step 1

Preheat oven to 350 degrees F (175 degrees C).

Step 2

Cream together the butter, sugar, salt, nutmeg and egg yolk. Add the flour a little at a time until mixture is stiff.

Step 3

Place onto floured board and knead lightly until the dough begins to crack. Roll out 1/4 inch thickness and cut into desired shapes.

Step 4

Place on un-greased cookie sheet, decorate with colored sugar crystals and maraschino cherries.

Step 5

Bake for 10 minutes or until golden brown.

Nutrition Facts

Per Serving:

282.8 calories; protein 2.6g 5% DV; carbohydrates 33.1g 11% DV; fat 16g 25% DV; cholesterol 57.7mg 19% DV; sodium 207.3mg 8% DV.

Easy Chewy Ginger Cookies

Prep: 15 mins **Cook:** 15 mins **Additional:** 5 mins **Total:** 35 mins **Servings:** 26 **Yield:** 26 large cookies

Ingredients

- 4 ½ cups all-purpose flour
- 4 teaspoons ground ginger
- 2 teaspoons baking powder
- 1 ½ teaspoons ground cinnamon
- ¼ teaspoon salt
- 1 ½ cups butter, softened
- 2 cups white sugar
- 2 large eggs eggs
- ½ cup molasses
- ¾ cup white sugar

Directions

Step 1

Preheat oven to 350 degrees F (175 degrees C).

Step 2

Whisk flour, ginger, baking powder, cinnamon, and salt together in a bowl.

Step 3

Beat butter in a large bowl until creamy. Gradually beat in 2 cups sugar until light and fluffy. Add eggs, one at a time, beating well after each addition. Beat in molasses. Stir 1/2 of the flour mixture into butter mixture; add remaining flour mixture and stir until dough is just-combined.

Step 4

Pour 3/4 sugar into a shallow bowl. Roll dough into 2 inch balls and roll each ball in sugar to coat. Place sugar-coated dough balls 2 1/2-inches apart on a baking sheet.

Step 5

Bake in the preheated oven until cookies are light brown and puffed, 12 to 14 minutes. Cool on the baking sheet for 2 minutes before transferring cookies to a wire rack to cool completely.

Nutrition Facts

Per Serving:

279.8 calories; protein 2.9g 6% DV; carbohydrates 42.8g 14% DV; fat 11.2g 17% DV; cholesterol 42.5mg 14% DV; sodium 143.6mg 6% DV.

Perfect Double Chocolate Peanut Candy Cookies

Prep: 30 mins **Cook:** 10 mins **Additional:** 45 mins **Total:** 1 hr 25 mins **Servings:** 48 **Yield:** 4 dozen cookies

Ingredients

- ½ cup butter, softened
- ½ cup vegetable shortening
- ¾ cup white sugar
- ⅔ cup packed brown sugar
- 1 teaspoon vanilla extract
- 2 large eggs eggs
- ⅔ cup unsweetened cocoa powder

- 2 ¼ cups all-purpose flour
- 1 teaspoon baking soda
- ¼ teaspoon salt
- ¾ cup semi-sweet chocolate chips
- 1 ¼ cups candy-coated peanut butter pieces (such as Reese's Pieces), divided

Directions

Step 1

Preheat oven to 350 degrees F (175 degrees C). Line baking sheets with parchment paper.

Step 2

In a large bowl, beat the butter and shortening together with an electric mixer until well combined. Beat in the white and brown sugar until the mixture is creamy, then beat the vanilla extract and eggs, followed by the cocoa powder. Beat until the mixture is even in color. In another bowl, whisk together the flour, baking soda, and salt; stir the flour mixture into the cocoa mixture until the dough is thoroughly mixed. Stir in the chocolate chips and 3/4 cup of peanut butter candies. Reserve the rest of the candy pieces.

Step 3

Cover the bowl with plastic wrap, and refrigerate the cookie dough until chilled, at least 45 minutes. Drop dough by tablespoon onto the prepared baking sheets. Gently press a few more candy pieces into the top of each cookie.

Step 4

Bake in the preheated oven 8 to 9 minutes; cool on baking sheets for 1 to 2 minutes before finishing cooling on racks.

Mini Pecan Tarts

Servings: 24 **Yield:** 4 dozen

Ingredients

- ½ cup margarine
- ½ cup white sugar
- 2 large egg yolks egg yolks
- 1 teaspoon almond extract
- 2 cups sifted all-purpose flour

- ½ cup margarine
- ½ cup corn syrup
- 1 cup confectioners' sugar
- 1 cup chopped pecans

Directions

Step 1

Preheat oven to 400 degrees F (200 degrees C).

Step 2

In a large bowl, mix 1/2 cup margarine (NOT butter) and 1/2 cup sugar. Stir in egg yolks, almond extract, and sifted flour.

Step 3

Spray tiny muffin cups with non-stick spray. Press mixture evenly into tiny muffin cups. Bake for 8 to 10 minutes.

Step 4

To make Filling: Bring to a boil 1/2 cup margarine, corn syrup, and confectioner's sugar. Stir in chopped pecans.

Step 5

Spoon into shells no more than 1/2 way. Top with pecan halves. Bake in a 350 degrees F (180 degrees C) oven for 5 minutes.

Nutrition Facts

Per Serving:

194.7 calories; protein 1.8g 4% DV; carbohydrates 22.8g 7% DV; fat 11.2g 17% DV; cholesterol 17.1mg 6% DV; sodium 88.7mg 4% DV.

Crisp Anise Seed Butter Cookies

Prep: 20 mins **Cook:** 8 mins **Additional:** 32 mins **Total:** 1 hr **Servings:** 50 **Yield:** 50 cookies

Ingredients

- 4 cups all-purpose flour
- 1 tablespoon baking powder
- ⅛ teaspoon salt
- 1 cup butter, softened
- 1 cup white sugar
- 2 large eggs eggs
- 1 teaspoon vanilla extract
- 3 tablespoons anise seeds
- ¼ cup white sugar for decoration
- 1 teaspoon ground cinnamon

Directions

Step 1

Sift together the flour, baking powder and salt; set aside. In a large bowl, cream together the butter and 1 cup sugar until smooth. Beat in the eggs one at a time then stir in the vanilla. Gradually mix in the sifted ingredients and anise seeds until well blended. Cover and chill for several hours or overnight.

Step 2

Preheat the oven to 400 degrees F (200 degrees C). Grease cookie sheets. On a lightly floured surface, roll the dough out to 1/4 inch in thickness. Cut into desired shapes with cookie cutters. Place cookies 1 1/2 inches apart onto cookie sheets. Sprinkle the tops with a mixture of the remaining 1/4 cup of sugar and cinnamon.

Step 3

Bake for 8 to 10 minutes in the preheated oven, until light brown. Cool on baking sheets for a few minutes before removing to wire racks to cool completely. Happy Holidays!

Nutrition Facts

Per Serving:

93 calories; protein 1.4g 3% DV; carbohydrates 12.9g 4% DV; fat 4g 6% DV; cholesterol 17.2mg 6% DV; sodium 55.2mg 2% DV.

Martina Cookies

Prep: 15 mins **Cook:** 10 mins **Total:** 25 mins **Servings:** 60 **Yield:** 60 cookies

Ingredients

- 2 cups butter, softened
- 4 cups all-purpose flour
- 1 cup confectioners' sugar
- 2 teaspoons vanilla extract

Directions

Step 1

Preheat oven to 325 degrees F (165 degrees C). Line a baking sheet with parchment paper.

Step 2

Beat butter in a large bowl until creamy and fluffy. Mix flour, confectioners' sugar, and vanilla extract into the creamed butter to form a dough. Roll dough into walnut-sized balls and arrange on the prepared baking sheet. Press the dough balls with the bottom of a glass until dough is flattened to 1/2-inch thick.

Step 3

Bake in the preheated oven until cookies are light brown, 10 to 13 minutes.

Nutrition Facts

Per Serving:

93.1 calories; protein 0.9g 2% DV; carbohydrates 8.5g 3% DV; fat 6.2g 10% DV; cholesterol 16.3mg 5% DV; sodium 43.8mg 2% DV.

Fig Filling for Pastry

Prep: 25 mins **Cook:** 5 mins **Total:** 30 mins **Servings:** 24 **Yield:** 2 cups

Ingredients

- 1 pound dried figs
- 1 orange, zested
- ½ cup semisweet chocolate chips
- ¼ cup whiskey
- ½ cup chopped walnuts
- 1 teaspoon cinnamon
- ¼ cup maple sugar

Directions

Step 1

Remove stems from figs with scissors. Chop in food processor in batches.

Step 2

111

In a non-stick pan, combine chopped figs with orange zest, chocolate chips, whiskey, walnuts, maple syrup, and cinnamon. Heat over medium heat until chocolate melts, stirring frequently. Cool completely.

Nutrition Facts

Per Serving:

95.1 calories; protein 1.1g 2% DV; carbohydrates 16.9g 6% DV; fat 2.9g 5% DV; cholesterolmg; sodium 2.8mg.

White Chocolate and Macadamia Nut Cookies

Prep: 15 mins **Cook:** 15 mins **Total:** 30 mins **Servings:** 24 **Yield:** 2 dozen cookies

Ingredients

- 1 ¼ cups oatmeal
- ½ cup sweetened flaked coconut
- 1 cup flour
- ½ teaspoon baking powder
- ½ teaspoon baking soda
- ½ teaspoon salt
- ½ cup butter, softened

- ½ cup light brown sugar
- ½ cup white sugar
- 1 egg, at room temperature
- ½ teaspoon vanilla extract
- ½ cup white chocolate chips
- 3 ounces macadamia nuts, coarsely chopped

Directions

Step 1

Preheat the oven to 375 degrees F (190 degrees C). Line a baking sheet with parchment paper.

Step 2

Place oatmeal in a blender and process into a fine powder. Transfer to a large bowl and set aside.

Step 3

Place coconut in the blender and process until finely chopped. Add to the bowl with the oatmeal. Add flour, baking powder, baking soda, and salt to the bowl; mix well and set aside.

Step 4

Cream butter, brown sugar, and white sugar together in a bowl. Add egg and vanilla extract. Add butter mixture to the bowl with the flour mixture and mix well. Stir in white chocolate chips and macadamia nuts.

Step 5

Roll heaping tablespoons of dough into balls and place on the prepared baking sheet.

Step 6

Bake in the preheated oven until edges start to brown lightly, 12 to 14 minutes.

Nutrition Facts

Per Serving:

159 calories; protein 2g 4% DV; carbohydrates 18.9g 6% DV; fat 8.8g 14% DV; cholesterol 18.7mg 6% DV; sodium 125.2mg 5% DV.

Espresso Biscotti

Prep: 25 mins **Cook:** 1 hr **Total:** 1 hr 25 mins **Servings:** 24 **Yield:** 24 biscotti

Ingredients

- ¼ cup unsalted butter
- ¾ cup white sugar
- 3 large eggs eggs
- 1 teaspoon vanilla extract
- 3 ¼ cups pastry flour
- 1 teaspoon ground cinnamon
- 1 teaspoon baking powder
- 1 teaspoon instant espresso powder
- 2 teaspoons grated orange zest
- ½ cup chocolate chips
- ½ cup dried apricots
- ½ cup dried cranberries
- ½ cup slivered almonds
- 1 egg white, lightly beaten

Directions

Step 1

Preheat oven to 350 degrees F (175 degrees C). Grease a cookie sheet or line it with parchment paper.

Step 2

Cream together butter and sugar in a bowl until light and fluffy. Beat in eggs and vanilla.

Step 3

Sift together the flour, cinnamon, and baking powder in a separate bowl. Mix dry ingredients into the egg mixture. Stir in the espresso powder, orange zest, chocolate chips, dried apricots, dried cranberries and almonds.

Step 4

Shape dough into two equal logs approximately 12 inches long by 2 inches diameter. Place logs on baking sheet, and flatten out to about 1 inch thickness. Brush the log with egg wash.

Step 5

Bake in the preheated oven until edges are golden and the center is firm, about 35 to 40 minutes. Remove from oven to cool on the pans. When loaves are cool enough to handle, use a serrated knife to slice the loaves diagonally into 1/2 inch thick slices. Return the slices to the baking sheet.

Step 6

Reduce oven temperature to 325 degrees F (165 degrees C). Bake until they start turning light brown, 15 to 20 minutes. Cool completely, and store in an airtight container at room temperature.

Nutrition Facts

Per Serving:

150.5 calories; protein 3.3g 7% DV; carbohydrates 25.4g 8% DV; fat 5g 8% DV; cholesterol 28.3mg 9% DV; sodium 32.6mg 1% DV.

Springerle I

Servings: 60 **Yield:** 10 dozen

Ingredients

- 4 large eggs eggs
- 2 tablespoons butter
- 2 teaspoons baking powder
- ¼ teaspoon salt
- 2 cups white sugar
- 4 cups all-purpose flour
- ¼ cup anise seed

Directions

Step 1

Beat eggs in large mixing bowl until very light.

Step 2

Add sugar and butter. Cream together until light and fluffy.

Step 3

Sift flour, baking powder, and salt. Add dry ingredients and combine.

Step 4

Knead dough until smooth ... add more flour to get a smooth dough if necessary.

Step 5

Cover dough and allow to chill in refrigerator for at least 2 hours.

Step 6

Roll onto slightly floured board to 1/2 inch thickness. Then roll again with springerle roller to make designs. Cut at border. Sprinkle anise seed on clean tea towel and place cookies on this. Allow to stand overnight (don't cover) to dry.

Step 7

Bake 12 to 15 minutes at 325 degrees F (170 degrees C).

Step 8

Cool completely. Store in tight tin container ... the longer they are stored, the more anise flavor they take up.

Nutrition Facts

Per Serving:

65.9 calories; protein 1.4g 3% DV; carbohydrates 13.3g 4% DV; fat 0.9g 1% DV; cholesterol 13.4mg 5% DV; sodium 33.6mg 1% DV.

Old Fashioned Sugar Cookies in a Jar

Prep: 15 mins **Total:** 15 mins **Servings:** 24 **Yield:** 2 dozen

Ingredients

- 3 cups all-purpose flour
- 1 teaspoon baking powder
- 1 teaspoon baking soda
- ⅛ teaspoon salt
- 1 ½ cups white sugar

- 1 cup butter, softened
- 2 large eggs eggs
- 1 teaspoon vanilla extract
- ½ teaspoon lemon extract

Directions

Step 1

In a medium bowl, stir together the flour, baking powder, baking soda and salt; set aside. In a 1 quart large mouth jar, layer the sugar on the bottom and the flour mixture on top. Attach a tag with the following instructions:

Step 2

Empty the contents of the jar into a large bowl. Cut in 1 cup of softened butter until the mixture is crumbly. In a separate bowl, beat 2 eggs, 1 teaspoon vanilla and 1/2 teaspoon of lemon extract until light and fluffy. Pour into the dry ingredients and mix until well blended. Cover bowl and chill for 1 hour.

Step 3

Preheat oven to 350 degrees F (175 degrees C). On a lightly floured surface, roll the dough out to 1/4 inch in thickness. Cut into desired shapes with cookie cutters. Place cookies 1 1/2 inches apart onto cookie sheets.

Step 4

Bake for 10 to 12 minutes in the preheated oven, until edges begin to brown. You can decorate them with sugar before baking of frost after baking.

Nutrition Facts

Per Serving:

179.9 calories; protein 2.2g 4% DV; carbohydrates 24.5g 8% DV; fat 8.2g 13% DV; cholesterol 35.8mg 12% DV; sodium 140.2mg 6% DV.

Nanaimo Bars II

Prep: 30 mins **Cook:** 10 mins **Additional:** 6 hrs 30 mins **Total:** 7 hrs 10 mins **Servings:** 16 **Yield:** 1 - 9x9 inch pan

Ingredients

- ½ cup butter
- 2 (1 ounce) squares semisweet chocolate
- ⅓ cup white sugar
- 1 ½ tablespoons pasteurized egg
- 1 cup rolled oats
- 1 ½ cups flaked coconut
- ½ cup chopped walnuts

- 1 teaspoon vanilla extract
- 2 cups confectioners' sugar
- 3 tablespoons butter, softened
- ½ teaspoon vanilla extract
- 2 ½ tablespoons milk
- 1 tablespoon butter
- 2 (1 ounce) squares semisweet chocolate

Directions

Step 1

In a saucepan, melt 1/2 cup butter or margarine with 2 squares chocolate. Remove from the heat, and stir in white sugar, egg, rolled oats, coconut, chopped nuts, and 1 teaspoon vanilla extract. Press mixture into a greased 9 inch square pan, and chill for 1 hour.

Step 2

Combine confectioners' sugar with 3 tablespoons softened butter, 1/2 teaspoon of the vanilla, and milk. Mix until it has an icing-like consistency, and spread it over the oat mixture in the pan. Chill for 1/2 hour.

Step 3

Melt remaining 1 tablespoon butter or margarine with remaining 2 squares chocolate. Spread over the top of the bars. Chill for 4 to 5 hours.

Step 4

Cut into squares using a hot knife; dip knife in hot water, and let it melt through the chocolate.

Nutrition Facts

Per Serving:

265.5 calories; protein 2.3g 5% DV; carbohydrates 30.8g 10% DV; fat 15.8g 24% DV; cholesterol 28.4mg 10% DV; sodium 84.6mg 3% DV.

Almond Butter Cookies

Servings: 36 **Yield:** 3 dozen cookies

Ingredients

- Cooking spray
- ¾ cup all purpose flour
- ½ cup whole wheat pastry flour, or regular whole wheat flour
- ¾ teaspoon salt
- 1 teaspoon baking soda
- ¼ cup unsalted butter, softened
- ¾ cup smooth, unsalted almond butter
- ⅓ cup packed light brown sugar
- ⅓ cup granulated sugar
- ½ teaspoon vanilla extract
- 1 egg
- 36 almonds raw whole almonds

Directions

Step 1

Preheat the oven to 375 degrees. Spray two baking sheets with cooking spray. In a large bowl whisk together the flours, salt and baking soda. In another large bowl beat together the butter, almond butter and sugars until fluffy. Add the vanilla and egg and beat until well combined. Gradually stir in the flour mixture, blending well.

Step 2

Shape the dough into 3/4 inch balls, and place on the baking sheets. Place an almond in center of each cookie and press down lightly. Bake for 10-12 minutes, until lightly browned. Cool on a wire rack.

Plum Jam Cookies

Servings: 24 **Yield:** 4 dozen

Ingredients

- 8 ounces butter
- 1 cup packed brown sugar
- 1 egg
- 1 teaspoon baking soda
- ¼ cup water
- 3 cups all-purpose flour
- 1 pinch salt
- 1 teaspoon baking powder
- 1 cup plum preserves

Directions

Step 1

Preheat oven to 375 degrees F(190 degrees C).

Step 2

In a large bowl, cream together the butter and brown sugar. Beat in the egg and water. Sift together the flour, baking powder, and salt; stir into the butter mixture until well blended.

Step 3

On a lightly floured surface, roll out the dough to 1/4 inch thickness. Cut with a 2 inch round cookie cutter. Put half of the cookies onto a cookie sheet and spread 1/2 of a teaspoon of plum jam in the center of each one. With a thimble, or small cookie cutter , cut the center out of the remaining cookies. Place these on top of the jam topped cookies to make sandwiches. Press together. Bake cookies for 10 minutes then remove to a rack to cool.

Nutrition Facts

Per Serving:

197.1 calories; protein 2g 4% DV; carbohydrates 30.2g 10% DV; fat 7.9g 12% DV; cholesterol 27.8mg 9% DV; sodium 132.3mg 5% DV.

Easy Toffee Bars

Prep: 5 mins **Cook:** 15 mins **Total:** 20 mins **Servings:** 24 **Yield:** 24 servings

Ingredients

- 1 cup butter
- 1 cup packed brown sugar
- 1 (10 ounce) package saltine crackers
- 1 (12 ounce) package semisweet chocolate chips

Directions

Step 1

Preheat oven to 400 degrees F (200 degrees C).

Step 2

In a small saucepan over medium-high heat melt butter with brown sugar; bring to a boil and remove from heat.

Step 3

Arrange crackers (salt side up) on a jelly roll pan. Pour butter mixture over crackers.

Step 4

Bake in preheated oven for 5 minutes.

Step 5

Remove from oven and sprinkle chocolate chips over crackers. Bake for another 5 minutes.

Nutrition Facts

Per Serving:

219.6 calories; protein 1.8g 4% DV; carbohydrates 26.1g 8% DV; fat 13.2g 20% DV; cholesterol 20.3mg 7% DV; sodium 183.7mg 7% DV.

Italian Frosted Chocolate Cookies

Prep: 1 hr **Cook:** 15 mins **Additional:** 8 hrs **Total:** 9 hrs 15 mins **Servings:** 120 **Yield:** 10 dozen cookies

Ingredients

- 7 cups all-purpose flour
- 2 cups white sugar
- 1 cup unsweetened cocoa powder (such as Hershey's)
- ¼ cup baking powder
- 1 ½ teaspoons ground cinnamon
- 1 ½ teaspoons ground cloves
- 1 ½ teaspoons ground allspice
- 1 teaspoon salt
- 1 large orange, zested
- ½ cup vegetable shortening (such as Crisco)
- ½ cup margarine (such as Parkay)
- 5 large eggs eggs
- 1 teaspoon vanilla extract, or to taste
- ¼ cup orange juice
- ¼ cup whole milk
- ½ (8 ounce) package cream cheese, softened
- ½ cup chopped walnuts
- 3 tablespoons whole milk, or more as needed
- 1 teaspoon orange juice, or as needed
- 3 cups confectioners' sugar, or more as needed

Directions

Step 1

Preheat oven to 350 degrees F (175 degrees C).

Step 2

Whisk flour, white sugar, cocoa powder, baking powder, cinnamon, cloves, allspice, and salt in a large bowl. Stir orange zest into flour mixture. Mix vegetable shortening and margarine into dry ingredients, using your hands, until mixture is crumbly.

Step 3

Beat eggs and vanilla extract in a bowl with an electric mixer until foamy; add egg mixture, 1/4 cup orange juice, and 1/4 cup milk to flour mixture and knead dough in the bowl until thoroughly combined and dough doesn't stick to your hands, about 8 minutes. Dough will be stiff. Knead cream cheese thoroughly into dough, followed by walnuts.

Step 4

Form dough into balls about 1 1/2 inches in diameter and place onto ungreased baking sheets.

Step 5

Bake cookies in the preheated oven until lightly browned, 12 to 14 minutes. Cool cookies on racks.

Step 6

Beat 3 tablespoons milk, 1 teaspoon orange juice, and 1 cup confectioners' sugar in a bowl until smooth; gradually beat in remaining confectioners' sugar until frosting is thick and drizzles slowly from a spoon.

Step 7

Dip tops of cookies into frosting and place frosted cookies on racks with waxed paper underneath to catch drips. Let cookies dry overnight.

Nutrition Facts

Per Serving:

78.1 calories; protein 1.3g 3% DV; carbohydrates 12.8g 4% DV; fat 2.7g 4% DV; cholesterol 8.8mg 3% DV; sodium 83.2mg 3% DV.

Cherry Shortbread Cookies

Servings: 12 **Yield:** 2 dozen

Ingredients

* 1 cup all-purpose flour
* ½ cup confectioners' sugar
* ½ cup cornstarch
* ½ cup chopped cherries
* 1 cup butter

Directions

Step 1

Preheat oven to 300 degrees F (150 degrees C).

Step 2

Cream butter and confectioners' sugar together. Add the cornstarch and flour and mix well. Stir in the chopped cherries. Drop teaspoonfuls of the dough onto a cookie sheet then press with tines of a floured fork.

Step 3

Bake at 300 degrees F (150 degrees C) until lightly golden, about 10 to 15 minutes.

Nutrition Facts

Per Serving:

217.7 calories; protein 1.3g 3% DV; carbohydrates 18.8g 6% DV; fat 15.5g 24% DV; cholesterol 40.7mg 14% DV; sodium 109.7mg 4% DV.

Granny's Strawberry Preserves-Filled Cookies

Prep: 1 hr **Cook:** 15 mins **Additional:** 2 hrs **Total:** 3 hrs 15 mins **Servings:** 36 **Yield:** 3 dozen cookies

Ingredients

- 1 cup shortening
- 1 cup white sugar
- 1 cup brown sugar
- ¼ cup milk
- 1 teaspoon vinegar
- 2 large eggs eggs
- 1 teaspoon vanilla extract

- 3 ½ cups all-purpose flour
- 1 teaspoon baking powder
- 1 teaspoon baking soda
- 1 teaspoon salt
- 1 teaspoon ground nutmeg
- 6 tablespoons strawberry preserves, or as needed

Directions

Step 1

Beat shortening, white sugar, and brown sugar in a bowl using an electric mixer until creamy and smooth.

Step 2

Mix milk and vinegar together and let stand 5 minutes to make 'sour milk'. Stir sour milk, eggs, and vanilla extract into shortening mixture.

Step 3

Sift flour, baking powder, baking soda, salt, and nutmeg together in a large bowl. Mix flour mixture into shortening mixture until incorporated. Refrigerate until fully chilled, 2 hours to overnight.

Step 4

Preheat oven to 350 degrees F (175 degrees C).

Step 5

Roll dough to a 1/8-inch thickness on a floured surface; cut into 2-inch rounds using a cookie cutter. Spoon 1 teaspoon preserves into the center of half the cookies; cover with remaining cookies. Lightly press edges of cookies together using a fork. Cut criss-cross slits into the top of each cookie using a knife. Arrange cookies on an ungreased baking sheet.

Step 6

Bake in the preheated oven until cookies are golden, 13 to 15 minutes.

Nutrition Facts

Per Serving:

153.3 calories; protein 1.7g 3% DV; carbohydrates 23.2g 8% DV; fat 6.2g 10% DV; cholesterol 10.5mg 4% DV; sodium 119.7mg 5% DV.

Reindeer Cookies

Prep: 30 mins **Cook:** 10 mins **Total:** 40 mins **Servings:** 36 **Yield:** 3 dozen cookies

Ingredients

- 1 cup butter, softened
- 1 cup white sugar
- 1 cup smooth peanut butter
- 2 large eggs eggs
- 1 teaspoon vanilla extract
- ½ teaspoon salt
- 3 cups all-purpose flour
- 2 teaspoons baking soda
- 72 eaches small pretzel twists, or as needed
- ½ cup chocolate chips, or as needed

Directions

Step 1

Preheat oven to 375 degrees F (190 degrees C).

Step 2

Beat butter, sugar, peanut butter, eggs, vanilla extract, and salt together in a bowl until smooth and creamy. Stir flour and baking soda into creamed butter mixture until well incorporated.

Step 3

Roll dough into 36 balls. Flatten each ball and shape into an upside-down triangle. Press two pretzels into the two top corners of each triangle for the antlers. Press two chocolate chips into the center of each triangle for the eyes, and one chocolate chip or M&M on the bottom of the triangle for the nose. Arrange cookies on baking sheets.

Step 4

Bake in the preheated oven until cookies are golden brown, 10 to 15 minutes.

Nutrition Facts

Per Serving:

208 calories; protein 4.5g 9% DV; carbohydrates 25.9g 8% DV; fat 10.2g 16% DV; cholesterol 23.9mg 8% DV; sodium 381.6mg 15% DV.

Grandma's Corn Flake Coconut Macaroons

Prep: 10 mins **Cook:** 20 mins **Additional:** 15 mins **Total:** 45 mins **Servings:** 30 **Yield:** 30 cookies

Ingredients

- 1 egg white
- ½ cup white sugar
- ¼ teaspoon salt
- ½ teaspoon vanilla extract
- ½ cup shredded coconut
- 1 cup cornflakes cereal

Directions

Step 1

Preheat oven to 300 degrees F (150 degrees C).

Step 2

Grease a baking sheet.

Step 3

Beat egg white in a bowl with an electric hand-mixer until stiff peaks form.

Step 4

Gradually beat sugar, 1 tablespoon at a time, into egg whites until fully incorporated. Stir salt and vanilla extract into egg whites until thoroughly mixed.

Step 5

Fold coconut and corn flakes into the mixture.

Step 6

Drop coconut mixture by the teaspoon onto the prepared baking sheet.

Step 7

Bake cookies in the preheated oven until lightly crisp, 20 minutes.

Step 8

Transfer cookies to wire rack to cool, at least 15 minutes.

Nutrition Facts

Per Serving:

22.6 calories; protein 0.2g; carbohydrates 4.8g 2% DV; fat 0.4g 1% DV; cholesterolmg; sodium 31.5mg 1% DV.

Eggnog Cookies I

Servings: 36 **Yield:** 2 to 3 dozen

Ingredients

- 1 cup butter, softened
- 2 cups white sugar
- 1 teaspoon vanilla extract
- 4 large eggs eggs
- 3 cups all-purpose flour
- 2 teaspoons baking powder
- ½ teaspoon salt
- ½ teaspoon ground nutmeg

Directions

Step 1

In a medium bowl, cream together the butter, sugar, and vanilla. Beat in eggs, one at a time. Sift together the flour, baking powder, salt and nutmeg; gradually stir into creamed mixture. Cover and refrigerate until firm.

Step 2

Preheat oven to 375 degrees F (190 degrees C).

Step 3

Drop by heaping spoonfuls onto an unprepared cookie sheet. Bake for 6 to 8 minutes in the preheated oven. Cookies should be lightly browned.

Nutrition Facts

Per Serving:

134.8 calories; protein 1.8g 4% DV; carbohydrates 19.2g 6% DV; fat 5.8g 9% DV; cholesterol 34.2mg 11% DV; sodium 103.7mg 4% DV.

Snow Flakes

Prep: 20 mins **Cook:** 10 mins **Additional:** 30 mins **Total:** 1 hr **Servings:** 72 **Yield:** 6 dozen

Ingredients

- 1 cup butter flavored shortening
- 1 (3 ounce) package cream cheese, softened
- 1 cup white sugar
- 1 egg yolk
- 1 teaspoon vanilla extract

- 1 teaspoon orange zest
- 2 ½ cups all-purpose flour
- ½ teaspoon salt
- ¼ teaspoon ground cinnamon

Directions

Step 1

Preheat oven to 350 degrees F (175 degrees C).

Step 2

In a medium bowl, cream together shortening, cream cheese, and sugar. Beat in egg yolk, vanilla, and orange zest. Continue beating until light and fluffy. Gradually stir in flour, salt, and cinnamon. Fill the cookie press, and form cookies on ungreased cookie sheet.

Step 3

Bake in preheated oven for 10 to 12 minutes. Remove from cookie sheet, and cool on wire racks.

Nutrition Facts

Per Serving:

57.9 calories; protein 0.6g 1% DV; carbohydrates 6.1g 2% DV; fat 3.5g 5% DV; cholesterol 4.1mg 1% DV; sodium 19.8mg 1% DV.

Oatmeal Thumbprints

Servings: 30 **Yield:** 5 dozen

Ingredients

- ½ cup butter, softened
- ½ cup shortening
- 1 cup packed brown sugar
- ¾ cup white sugar
- 2 large eggs eggs
- 2 ½ cups all-purpose flour
- 1 teaspoon baking soda

- 1 teaspoon salt
- ½ teaspoon ground cinnamon
- ½ cup water
- 2 ½ cups quick cooking oats
- ½ cup finely chopped walnuts
- 1 teaspoon almond extract
- ¼ cup raspberry jam

Directions

Step 1

Preheat oven to 400 degrees F (205 degrees C).

Step 2

Cream butter and shortening with sugars. Beat in eggs. In a separate bowl, sift together flour, baking soda, salt, nuts and cinnamon. Add to butter mixture alternately with water. Stir in oats and almond extract.

Step 3

Drop by teaspoons on ungreased cookie sheets. Make a small indentation in each cookie. Fill with preserves.

Step 4

Bake for 10-12 minutes.

Nutrition Facts

Per Serving:

193.5 calories; protein 2.7g 6% DV; carbohydrates 26.9g 9% DV; fat 8.7g 13% DV; cholesterol 20.5mg 7% DV; sodium 148.8mg 6% DV.

Pistachio Cream Cheese Fingers

Prep: 30 mins **Cook:** 12 mins **Additional:** 1 hr 3 mins **Total:** 1 hr 45 mins **Servings:** 100 **Yield:** 8 dozen

Ingredients

- 1 cup butter, softened
- 1 cup white sugar
- 1 (8 ounce) package cream cheese, softened
- 1 egg
- 1 teaspoon vanilla extract
- 2 ¼ cups all-purpose flour

- 1 (3 ounce) package instant pistachio pudding mix
- 1 teaspoon baking powder
- ½ teaspoon salt
- 3 (1 ounce) squares semisweet chocolate
- 1 teaspoon shortening

Directions

Step 1

In a large bowl, cream together the butter, sugar, and cream cheese until light and fluffy. Beat in the egg and vanilla. Combine the flour, dry pudding mix, baking powder, and salt; stir into the creamed mixture. Cover dough, and refrigerate for at least one hour for easier handling.

Step 2

Preheat oven to 350 degrees F (175 degrees C). Grease cookie sheets. Shape teaspoonfuls of dough into finger shapes, about 1 1/2 inches long. Place cookies on prepared cookie sheets.

Step 3

Bake for 9 to 12 minutes in the preheated oven, or until set and very lightly browned on bottoms. Cool completely on a wire rack.

Step 4

In small saucepan over low heat, melt together chocolate and shortening, stirring constantly until smooth and well blended. Drizzle a small amount of chocolate over each cookie. Allow the chocolate to set before storing.

Nutrition Facts

Per Serving:

51.5 calories; protein 0.6g 1% DV; carbohydrates 5.6g 2% DV; fat 3g 5% DV; cholesterol 9.2mg 3% DV; sodium 51.1mg 2% DV.

Cookie in a Jar

Prep: 20 mins **Total:** 20 mins **Servings:** 12 **Yield:** 2 1/2 dozen

Ingredients

- ½ cup white chocolate chips
- ½ cup crispy rice cereal
- 1 ½ cups all-purpose flour
- ¾ teaspoon baking soda
- ¼ teaspoon baking powder
- ½ cup packed brown sugar
- ½ cup semisweet chocolate chips
- ½ cup rolled oats
- ½ cup white sugar

Directions

Step 1

In a 1 quart jar, layer the ingredients in the order listed. Pack down firmly after each addition.

Step 2

Attach a tag with the following instructions: Cookie in a Jar 1. Preheat the oven to 350 degrees F (175 degrees C). 2. In a large bowl, cream 1/2 cup margarine until light and fluffy. Mix in 1 egg and 2 tablespoons water. Add the entire contents of the jar, and stir until well blended. Drop by rounded spoonfuls onto an ungreased cookie sheet. 3. Bake for 10 to 12 minutes in preheated oven. Remove from baking sheets to cool on wire racks.

Nutrition Facts

Per Serving:

216.8 calories; protein 3g 6% DV; carbohydrates 41.2g 13% DV; fat 5.1g 8% DV; cholesterol 1.6mg 1% DV; sodium 109.5mg 4% DV.

Vanille Kipferl I

Prep: 30 mins **Cook:** 8 mins **Additional:** 2 mins **Total:** 40 mins **Servings:** 18 **Yield:** 3 dozen

Ingredients

- 2 cups all-purpose flour
- ⅓ cup white sugar
- ¾ cup ground almonds

- 1 cup unsalted butter
- ¼ cup vanilla sugar
- ¼ cup confectioners' sugar

Directions

Step 1

Preheat oven to 325 degrees F (170 degrees C). Line a baking sheet with parchment paper.

Step 2

Combine flour, 1/3 cup sugar, and ground almonds. Cut in butter with pastry blender, then quickly knead into a dough.

Step 3

Shape dough into logs and cut off 1/2-inch pieces. Shape each piece into a crescent and place on prepared baking sheet.

Step 4

Bake in preheated oven until edges are golden brown, 8 to 10 minutes. Cool 1 minute and carefully roll in vanilla sugar mixture.

Nutrition Facts

Per Serving:

207 calories; protein 2.8g 6% DV; carbohydrates 20g 6% DV; fat 13.4g 21% DV; cholesterol 27.1mg 9% DV; sodium 1.8mg.

Cake Mix Gingerbread Men

Prep: 30 mins **Cook:** 10 mins **Additional:** 2 hrs 20 mins **Total:** 3 hrs **Servings:** 12 **Yield:** 12 servings

Ingredients

- 1 package Duncan Hines Moist Deluxe Spice Cake Mix
- 1 cup all-purpose flour
- 2 large eggs eggs
- ⅓ cup vegetable oil
- ⅓ cup dark molasses
- 2 teaspoons ground ginger
- non-pareils
- 1 tub Duncan Hines Creamy Home-Style Vanilla Icing
- heavy weight storage or freezer bag

Directions

Step 1

Preheat oven to 375 degrees F.

Step 2

Combine cake mix, flour, eggs, oil, molasses and ginger in large bowl (mixture will be soft). Refrigerate 2 hours.

Step 3

Place dough on lightly floured surface, cover with waxed paper. Roll dough to 1/4-inch thickness. Cut with gingerbread man cookie cutter. Place 3 inches apart on ungreased cookie sheet. Decorate with non pareils.

Step 4

Bake 8 to 10 minutes or until edges start to brown. Remove immediately to cooling rack.

Step 5

Place icing in storage bag. Snip just the tip of one corner off to allow for a small hole. Pipe the face and ruffles onto cookies.

Nutrition Facts

Per Serving:

454.2 calories; protein 3.2g 6% DV; carbohydrates 74.3g 24% DV; fat 17g 26% DV; cholesterol 31mg 10% DV; sodium 360.5mg 14% DV.

Cherry Mash Bars

Prep: 30 mins **Cook:** 30 mins **Total:** 1 hr **Servings:** 16 **Yield:** 1 - 9x9 inch pan

Ingredients

- 2 tablespoons butter
- 1 cup white sugar
- ¼ teaspoon salt
- ⅓ cup half-and-half cream
- 1 cup miniature marshmallows

- 1 cup cherry baking chips
- 1 cup semisweet chocolate chips
- ½ cup peanut butter
- 1 cup roasted Spanish peanuts

Directions

Step 1

Line an 8x8 or 9x9 inch square pan with waxed paper.

Step 2

In a medium saucepan, combine butter, sugar, salt and half and half. Heat until boiling, stirring occasionally. Boil for 5 minutes, stirring enough to keep from scorching. Remove from heat and stir in the marshmallows, and cherry chips. Press the mixture into the prepared pan.

Step 3

In the microwave or in a metal bowl over a pan of simmering water, melt chocolate chips, and peanut butter together stirring frequently until smooth. Spread over the mixture in the pan. Refrigerate for 2 hours before cutting into squares.

Nutrition Facts

Per Serving:

285.7 calories; protein 5.9g 12% DV; carbohydrates 32.1g 10% DV; fat 16.5g 25% DV; cholesterol 5.7mg 2% DV; sodium 130.5mg 5% DV.

Cranberry Cornmeal Linzer Cookies

Prep: 45 mins **Cook:** 10 mins **Additional:** 1 hr **Total:** 1 hr 55 mins **Servings:** 42 **Yield:** 42 servings

Ingredients

Cookies:

- ¾ cup butter, softened
- ¾ cup white sugar
- 1 egg
- 1 ½ cups all-purpose flour
- ½ cup cornmeal
- 1 teaspoon baking powder
- ⅜ teaspoon salt
- 1 teaspoon vanilla extract

Filling:

- 1 ½ cups finely chopped cranberries
- ⅓ cup brown sugar
- ⅓ cup water
- 1 ½ tablespoons butter
- 1 ½ tablespoons lemon juice

Directions

Step 1

Beat 3/4 cup butter and and white sugar together in a bowl with an electric mixer until creamy. Beat egg into butter mixture.

Step 2

Whisk flour, cornmeal, baking powder, and salt together in a bowl. Gradually add flour mixture to butter mixture; stir. Beat vanilla into butter mixture. Form dough into a ball, wrap tightly in plastic wrap, and refrigerate until firm, at least 1 hour.

Step 3

Preheat oven to 350 degrees F (175 degrees C). Lightly grease baking sheets.

Step 4

Roll dough out onto a lightly floured surface to 1/8-inch thick. Cut dough with a round or Linzer cookie cutter. Use a smaller cutter to cut the center from the tops. Place cookie bottoms and tops 1-inch apart on prepared baking sheets.

Step 5

Bake in the preheated oven until edges are lightly golden, 10 to 12 minutes. Transfer to wire racks to cool.

Step 6

Stir cranberries, brown sugar, and water together in a saucepan over medium-high heat; cook until cranberries are soft, about 10 minutes. Stir butter and lemon juice into cranberry mixture; remove from heat and cool.

Step 7

Spread a small amount of the cranberry mixture onto one side of the bottom half of a cookie. Place the top half of the cookie on top of the cranberry mixture. Repeat assembly process with remaining cookies and cranberry filling.

Nutrition Facts

Per Serving:

78.7 calories; protein 0.8g 2% DV; carbohydrates 10.4g 3% DV; fat 3.9g 6% DV; cholesterol 14.2mg 5% DV; sodium 61.5mg 3% DV.

Moravian Ginger Cookies I

Servings: 30 **Yield:** 5 dozen

Ingredients

- 3 tablespoons shortening
- 2 tablespoons brown sugar
- ⅓ cup molasses
- 1 ¼ cups all-purpose flour
- ¼ teaspoon baking soda
- ½ teaspoon salt
- ¼ teaspoon ground cinnamon
- ¼ teaspoon ground ginger
- ¼ teaspoon ground cloves
- 1 pinch ground nutmeg
- 1 dash ground allspice

Directions

Step 1

In a medium bowl, cream together the shortening, brown sugar and molasses until smooth. Sift together the flour, baking soda, salt, cinnamon, ginger, cloves, nutmeg and allspice; blend into the creamed mixture. Work dough with hands until well blended. Cover and chill for about 4 hours. Dough must be thoroughly chilled to hold together.

Step 2

Preheat oven to 375 degrees F (190 degrees C). Roll out dough paper thin a little at a time. Cut into desired shapes using cookie cutters. Place on greased baking sheets.

Step 3

Bake 5 to 6 minutes in the preheated oven, or until lightly browned.

Nutrition Facts

Per Serving:

44.7 calories; protein 0.5g 1% DV; carbohydrates 7.7g 3% DV; fat 1.4g 2% DV; cholesterolmg; sodium 51mg 2% DV.

Rosemary Slices

Prep: 25 mins **Cook:** 10 mins **Additional:** 2 hrs 15 mins **Total:** 2 hrs 50 mins **Servings:** 60 **Yield:** 5 dozen cookies

Ingredients

- ½ cup butter, softened
- ¾ cup white sugar
- 1 medium egg
- 1 cup whole wheat flour
- ¾ cup all-purpose flour
- 1 tablespoon finely chopped fresh rosemary
- ½ teaspoon baking powder

Directions

Step 1

Beat the butter and sugar together in a bowl until creamy and smooth, and stir in the egg until well incorporated. Stir in the whole wheat flour, all-purpose flour, rosemary, and baking powder until well blended. Cut the dough into 2 equal-sized pieces, and shape each piece into a log about 1 1/4-inch in diameter. Wrap the logs in plastic wrap, and refrigerate at least 2 hours, or place in freezer for about 1 hour.

Step 2

Preheat an oven to 350 degrees F (175 degrees C). Line baking sheets with parchment paper.

Step 3

Cut the logs of dough into thin slices, 1/8 to 1/4-inch thick. Place the slices on the prepared baking sheets, and bake in the preheated oven until the cookies are set and the edges turn golden brown, 10 to 12 minutes. Cool for 1 minute on baking sheets before removing to wire racks to finish cooling.

Nutrition Facts

Per Serving:

37 calories; protein 0.6g 1% DV; carbohydrates 5.2g 2% DV; fat 1.7g 3% DV; cholesterol 7.2mg 2% DV; sodium 16.3mg 1% DV.

Kourambiedes III

Servings: 18 **Yield:** 3 dozen

Ingredients

- 1 cup unsalted butter
- 4 tablespoons confectioners' sugar
- 1 teaspoon vanilla extract
- 2 cups sifted all-purpose flour
- 1 cup chopped pecans
- 36 eaches whole cloves
- ½ cup confectioners' sugar

Directions

Step 1

Preheat oven to 350 degrees F (175 degrees C).

Step 2

In a medium bowl, cream the butter and confectioners' sugar together. Stir in the vanilla, then the flour, then the pecans.

Step 3

Roll dough into walnut sized balls and insert a clove into each one. Place on an unprepared cookie sheet and bake for 15 to 18 minutes in the preheated oven. Roll the cookies in powdered sugar while they are still hot. Remove cloves before serving or warn guests to remove them.

Nutrition Facts

Per Serving:

209.5 calories; protein 2.2g 5% DV; carbohydrates 17.7g 6% DV; fat 14.8g 23% DV; cholesterol 27.1mg 9% DV; sodium 7.1mg.

Great Grandad's Sugar Cookies

Prep: 30 mins **Cook:** 10 mins **Additional:** 30 mins **Total:** 1 hr 10 mins **Servings:** 30 **Yield:** 5 dozen

Ingredients

- 6 cups all-purpose flour
- 1 tablespoon baking powder
- 1 teaspoon ground nutmeg
- 1 pinch salt
- 2 ½ cups white sugar
- 1 ½ cups shortening
- 1 teaspoon baking soda
- 1 cup sour milk
- 3 large eggs eggs, beaten
- 1 teaspoon vanilla extract

Directions

Step 1

Preheat oven to 350 degrees F (175 degrees C). Line cookie sheets with parchment paper.

Step 2

In a medium bowl, stir together 4 cups flour, baking powder, nutmeg, salt, and sugar. Cut in the shortening until the mixture resembles coarse crumbs. Stir in baking soda, sour milk, beaten eggs, and vanilla. Stir as little as possible, and add the remaining flour as necessary to make dough thick enough to roll out.

Step 3

On a lightly floured surface, roll out dough 1/4 inch thick. Cut into desired shapes with cookie cutters. Place cookies 1 inch apart on the prepared cookie sheets.

Step 4

Bake for 8 to 10 minutes in preheated oven. Cool on baking sheets.

Nutrition Facts

Per Serving:

257.7 calories; protein 3.5g 7% DV; carbohydrates 36.4g 12% DV; fat 11.1g 17% DV; cholesterol 18.9mg 6% DV; sodium 106.8mg 4% DV.

German Oatmeal Date Cookies

Prep: 20 mins **Cook:** 20 mins **Additional:** 20 mins **Total:** 1 hr **Servings:** 50 **Yield:** 50 cookies

Ingredients

- 10 tablespoons unsalted butter, divided
- 3 cups rolled oats
- 2 large eggs eggs
- ½ cup white sugar
- 1 teaspoon vanilla sugar
- 1 teaspoon baking powder
- 1 ½ cups finely chopped, pitted dates

Directions

Step 1

Melt 9 tablespoons butter in a small saucepan over low heat; mix in oats. Remove from heat and let cool, about 20 minutes.

Step 2

Mix eggs, sugar, vanilla sugar, and baking powder together in a large bowl; stir in dates-oat mixture.

Step 3

Preheat oven to 350 degrees F (175 degrees C). Grease a baking sheet with remaining 1 tablespoon butter.

Step 4

Use 2 teaspoons to place little mounds of oat-date mixture 2 inches apart onto the baking sheets.

Step 5

Bake in the preheated oven until lightly browned on the top and bottom, about 20 minutes.

Nutrition Facts

Per Serving:

62.2 calories; protein 1g 2% DV; carbohydrates 8.7g 3% DV; fat 2.8g 4% DV; cholesterol 13.5mg 5% DV; sodium 29.3mg 1% DV.

Ricciarelli

Prep: 40 mins **Cook:** 7 mins **Additional:** 13 hrs **Total:** 13 hrs 47 mins **Servings:** 20 **Yield:** 20 cookies

Ingredients

- 2 ¼ cups white sugar
- 2 cups blanched almonds
- ½ cup egg whites

- 1 drop vanilla extract
- ¼ cup confectioners' sugar, or as needed
- 2 tablespoons all-purpose flour

Directions

Step 1

Combine white sugar and almonds in the bowl of a food processor; pulse into a fine powder. Pour into a bowl.

Step 2

Combine 1/4 cup egg whites and vanilla extract in a bowl; add to almond-sugar mixture, mixing as little as possible. Wrap dough in plastic wrap and refrigerate for 12 hours.

Step 3

Line a baking sheet with parchment paper.

Step 4

Remove dough from fridge. Sift 2 tablespoons confectioners' sugar and flour onto a clean work surface. Place dough in the center and add remaining 1/4 cup egg whites. Knead egg whites into dough until soft and smooth, adding additional confectioners' sugar and flour as needed.

Step 5

Roll portions of dough into 1-inch-thick logs. Take walnut-sized dough pieces from each log and shape into diamonds with slightly wet hands. Place cookies on the prepared baking sheet and generously dust with confectioner's sugar. Let rest at room temperature for 1 to 2 hours.

Step 6

Preheat oven to 350 degrees F (175 degrees C).

Step 7

Bake cookies in the preheated oven until lightly golden, 7 to 8 minutes. Cool on the baking sheet before serving.

Nutrition Facts

Per Serving:

183.3 calories; protein 3.9g 8% DV; carbohydrates 27.6g 9% DV; fat 7.3g 11% DV; cholesterolmg; sodium 14.2mg 1% DV.

Peanut Butter Dreams

Servings: 60 Yield: 4 to 5 dozen

Ingredients

- ½ cup butter
- 4 cups confectioners' sugar
- 2 cups creamy peanut butter

- 3 cups crisp rice cereal
- 2 cups semisweet chocolate chips
- 4 tablespoons shortening

Directions

Step 1

In a large mixing bowl, mix butter, sugar, peanut butter and crisp rice cereal together thoroughly.

Step 2

Roll into small balls and set aside.

Step 3

Melt chocolate chips and shortening in a small saucepan over low heat. Remove from heat. Coat the small balls in the chocolate mixture. Refrigerate for several hours.

Nutrition Facts

Per Serving:

137.6 calories; protein 2.7g 5% DV; carbohydrates 14.9g 5% DV; fat 8.4g 13% DV; cholesterol 4.1mg 1% DV; sodium 61.1mg 2% DV.

Polish Christmas Cookies

Servings: 72 **Yield:** 5 to 6 dozen

Ingredients

- 1 cup butter
- 1 cup shortening
- 2 cups white sugar
- 5 large eggs eggs

- 7 ½ cups all-purpose flour
- 6 teaspoons baking powder
- ½ teaspoon salt
- ½ ounce anise extract

Directions

Step 1

Preheat oven to 350 degrees F (175 degrees C).

Step 2

Cream the butter, shortening and the sugar together. Stir in the eggs and continue to beat. Add the anise flavoring. Stir in 7 cups of the flour, the baking powder and the salt. Mix until the dough is soft. Add the additional cup of flour if needed. Chill the dough.

Step 3

On a lightly floured surface roll out the dough and cut with cookie cutters. Place cookies on greased cookie sheets.

Step 4

Bake at 350 degrees F (175 degrees C) for 12 to 15 minutes. Frost and decorate when cookies are cooled.

Nutrition Facts

Per Serving:

122.3 calories; protein 1.8g 4% DV; carbohydrates 15.6g 5% DV; fat 5.9g 9% DV; cholesterol 19.7mg 7% DV; sodium 80.1mg 3% DV.

Chocolate Chip Cookies with Peppermint Extract

Prep: 20 mins **Cook:** 10 mins **Additional:** 1 min **Total:** 31 mins **Servings:** 48 **Yield:** 4 dozen cookies

Ingredients

- 1 cup unsalted butter, softened
- 1 cup white sugar
- 1 cup packed light brown sugar
- 2 large eggs eggs
- 2 teaspoons vanilla extract
- 1 teaspoon peppermint extract
- 1 teaspoon baking soda

- 2 teaspoons hot water
- 3 cups all-purpose flour
- 1 teaspoon salt
- ½ teaspoon cream of tartar
- 2 cups semisweet chocolate chips
- 10 drops green food coloring, or more to taste

Directions

Step 1

Preheat oven to 350 degrees F (175 degrees C).

Step 2

Combine butter, white sugar, and brown sugar in a large bowl; beat with an electric mixer until creamy. Beat in eggs. Stir in vanilla extract and peppermint extract. Dissolve baking soda in hot water and mix into the batter.

Step 3

Combine flour, salt, and cream of tartar in a separate bowl. Add to the batter gradually; mix well. Stir in chocolate chips.

Step 4

Drop spoonfuls of batter onto ungreased baking sheets.

Step 5

Bake in the preheated oven until edges are nicely browned, about 10 minutes. Cool on the baking sheets for 1 minute; transfer to a wire rack to cool completely.

Nutrition Facts

Per Serving:

133.2 calories; protein 1.4g 3% DV; carbohydrates 19.1g 6% DV; fat 6.2g 10% DV; cholesterol 17.9mg 6% DV; sodium 80.3mg 3% DV.

Chocolate Orange Cookies

Prep: 30 mins **Cook:** 10 mins **Additional:** 10 mins **Total:** 50 mins **Servings:** 36 **Yield:** 3 dozen

Ingredients

- 1 (1 ounce) square unsweetened chocolate
- ¾ cup butter
- ¾ cup white sugar
- 1 egg
- 1 teaspoon vanilla extract
- 1 ½ cups all-purpose flour
- 1 teaspoon baking powder
- 1 pinch salt
- 1 tablespoon orange zest

Directions

Step 1

Preheat the oven to 350 degrees F (175 degrees C). In a microwave-safe dish, melt the unsweetened chocolate, stirring frequently until smooth. Set aside.

Step 2

In a medium bowl, cream together the butter and sugar until smooth. Beat in the egg and vanilla. Combine the flour, baking powder, and salt; stir into the creamed mixture. Divide dough in two. Mix orange zest into one half, and melted chocolate into the other half. Use a bit of each mixture to form a ball about 1 inch in diameter.

Step 3

Bake for 8 to 10 minutes in the preheated oven, or until center is set. Cool on wire racks.

Nutrition Facts

Per Serving:

75.5 calories; protein 0.9g 2% DV; carbohydrates 8.5g 3% DV; fat 4.4g 7% DV; cholesterol 15.3mg 5% DV; sodium 47.3mg 2% DV.

Grandma's Molasses Ginger Cookies

Prep: 15 mins **Cook:** 15 mins **Additional:** 8 hrs **Total:** 8 hrs 30 mins **Servings:** 48 **Yield:** 48 cookies

Ingredients

- 1 ½ cups sugar, plus more for sprinkling
- 2 sticks butter, softened
- ¾ cup Grandma's Original Molasses
- 1 egg
- 1 teaspoon Spice Islands Pure Vanilla Extract
- 3 cups flour, plus more for dusting

- 1 teaspoon Clabber Girl Baking Soda
- 1 teaspoon Clabber Girl Baking Powder
- 1 teaspoon Spice Islands Ground Nutmeg
- 1 teaspoon Spice Islands Ground Cloves
- 1 tablespoon Spice Islands Ground Ginger
- 1 tablespoon Spice Islands Ground Saigon Cinnamon

Directions

Step 1

In a large bowl, whip together sugar, butter, molasses, egg, and vanilla. Mix in flour, baking soda, baking powder, and spices until dough comes together. Wrap well and refrigerate overnight.

Step 2

Preheat the oven to 350 degrees F.

Step 3

Roll cookie dough into 1-inch balls and roll in sugar to coat. Arrange on rimmed baking sheets. Bake for 15 minutes.

Cook's Note:

Substitute margarine for butter, if desired.

Nutrition Facts

Per Serving:

109.6 calories; protein 1g 2% DV; carbohydrates 17.9g 6% DV; fat 4g 6% DV; cholesterol 13.6mg 5% DV; sodium 47.2mg 2% DV.

No-Bake Haystacks

Prep: 10 mins **Cook:** 5 mins **Additional:** 15 mins **Total:** 30 mins **Servings:** 72 **Yield:** 6 dozen cookies

Ingredients

- 3 cups quick cooking oats
- 1 cup flaked coconut
- 1 cup roasted peanuts, chopped
- 1 cup raisins
- 2 cups white sugar
- ½ cup milk
- ¼ cup butter
- ¼ cup unsweetened cocoa powder
- 1 teaspoon vanilla

Directions

Step 1

Mix the oats, coconut, peanuts, and raisins together in a large bowl.

Step 2

Stir the sugar, milk, butter, and cocoa powder together in a saucepan and bring to a boil; boil for 1 minute and immediately remove from heat. Stir the vanilla into the cocoa mixture; pour over the oat mixture and stir to coat. Scoop heaping tablespoonfuls of the mixture and drop into haystack-like piles onto waxed paper; allow to cool completely before serving.

Nutrition Facts

Per Serving:

65 calories; protein 1.1g 2% DV; carbohydrates 10.9g 4% DV; fat 2.2g 3% DV; cholesterol 1.8mg 1% DV; sodium 25.2mg 1% DV.

Super Duper Chocolate Cookies

Prep: 20 mins **Cook:** 15 mins **Additional:** 3 hrs **Total:** 3 hrs 35 mins **Servings:** 48 **Yield:** 4 dozen

Ingredients

- 4 (1 ounce) squares unsweetened chocolate
- ½ cup vegetable shortening
- 2 cups white sugar
- 2 teaspoons vanilla extract
- 4 large eggs eggs
- 2 cups all-purpose flour
- 2 teaspoons baking powder
- ⅛ teaspoon salt

- ½ cup chopped walnuts
- ¾ cup confectioners' sugar

Directions

Step 1

Melt the chocolate and shortening in a saucepan over low heat. Remove from heat and mix in sugar and vanilla. Beat in eggs 1 at a time. In a bowl, sift together flour, baking powder and salt. Stir in the chocolate mixture and nuts. Chill dough in the refrigerator 3 hours or overnight.

Step 2

Preheat oven to 350 degrees F (175 degrees C). Grease cookie sheets.

Step 3

Place confectioners' sugar in a bowl. Roll dough into 1 inch balls. Roll dough balls in confectioners' sugar to coat. Arrange 3 inches apart on the prepared cookie sheets.

Step 4

Bake 12 to 15 minutes in the preheated oven. The cookies will look soft when removed from the oven. Transfer to a wire rack to cool. Enjoy!

Nutrition Facts

Per Serving:

104.2 calories; protein 1.6g 3% DV; carbohydrates 15.2g 5% DV; fat 4.6g 7% DV; cholesterol 15.5mg 5% DV; sodium 32.9mg 1% DV.

Cranberry-Orange Shortbread Cookies with Apricots

Prep: 20 mins **Cook:** 20 mins **Additional:** 4 hrs 30 mins **Total:** 5 hrs 10 mins **Servings:** 32 **Yield:** 32 cookies

Ingredients

- 1 ¾ cups all-purpose flour
- ¼ teaspoon baking powder
- ¼ teaspoon salt
- ¼ teaspoon ground nutmeg
- 1 cup unsalted butter, softened
- ½ cup white sugar
- 1 teaspoon vanilla extract
- 2 large oranges, zested
- 1 cup finely chopped dried cranberries
- ½ cup finely chopped dried apricots

Directions

Step 1

Combine flour, baking powder, salt, and nutmeg in a bowl; mix together.

Step 2

Cream butter in a large bowl using an electric blender until fluffy and lightened in color slightly. Add sugar and cream on medium-high speed until light and fluffy, several more minutes. Mix in vanilla and orange zest. Add flour mixture in 3 batches and mix until just combined, kneading the last addition by hand. Knead in cranberries and apricots.

Step 3

Divide dough in half and roll out into two 1 1/2x7-inch long logs. Wrap each log in parchment paper and refrigerate until dough is chilled, at least 4 hours.

Step 4

Preheat the oven to 350 degrees F (175 degrees C). Line 2 baking sheets with parchment paper.

Step 5

Remove dough from the refrigerator and cut each log into about 16 slices that are 1/3-inch thick. Place slices 1 inch apart on prepared baking sheets.

Step 6

Bake in the preheated oven until cookies just begin to turn slightly golden on bottom, 20 to 25 minutes. Cool on baking sheets for 5 minutes before removing to wire racks to cool completely. Store in an airtight container.

Nutrition Facts

Per Serving:

109.9 calories; protein 0.9g 2% DV; carbohydrates 14.1g 5% DV; fat 5.9g 9% DV; cholesterol 15.3mg 5% DV; sodium 23.1mg 1% DV.

Chocolate Spritz (Cookie Press)

Prep: 15 mins **Cook:** 10 mins **Total:** 25 mins **Servings:** 84 **Yield:** 84 cookies

Ingredients

- 1 ½ cups butter, softened
- 1 cup white sugar
- ¼ cup unsweetened cocoa powder

- 1 teaspoon baking powder
- 1 egg
- 1 teaspoon vanilla extract

- 3 ¼ cups all-purpose flour

Directions

Step 1

Preheat oven to 375 degrees F (190 degrees C).

Step 2

Beat butter in a large mixing bowl using an electric mixer until creamy; add sugar, cocoa powder, and baking powder. Beat until combined. Scrape sides of bowl down if needed. Stir egg and vanilla extract into butter mixture until just combined; mix in flour.

Step 3

Fill the cookie press with dough; press cookies onto an ungreased baking sheet.

Step 4

Bake in the preheated oven until edges of cookies are lightly browned, 8 to 10 minutes.

Nutrition Facts

Per Serving:

57.5 calories; protein 0.7g 1% DV; carbohydrates 6.2g 2% DV; fat 3.4g 5% DV; cholesterol 10.9mg 4% DV; sodium 30.1mg 1% DV.

Orange Meltaway Cookies

Prep: 30 mins **Cook:** 30 mins **Additional:** 30 mins **Total:** 1 hr 30 mins **Servings:** 45 **Yield:** 140 small cookies

Ingredients

- 2 cups all-purpose flour
- 1 teaspoon baking soda
- 1 teaspoon cream of tartar
- 1 cup butter
- 1 ½ cups sifted confectioners' sugar

- 1 teaspoon orange extract
- 1 tablespoon grated orange zest
- 1 beaten egg
- ½ cup confectioners' sugar, for dusting

Directions

Step 1

Preheat oven to 375 degrees F (190 degrees C). Line baking sheets with parchment paper, and set aside.

Step 2

Mix the flour, baking soda, and cream of tartar in a bowl. In another bowl, beat the butter and 1 1/2 cups confectioners' sugar together with an electric mixer until light and fluffy. Mix in orange extract, grated orange zest, and egg. Stir in the flour mixture, and blend well.

Step 3

Drop teaspoon-sized portions of dough about 2 inches apart onto the parchment lined baking sheets. The cookies will spread out to about 1 1/2 inches when baked.

Step 4

Bake in the preheated oven for 10 to 14 minutes, until the cookies are light brown. Remove from the oven, and sift remaining confectioners' sugar onto the hot cookies. Allow to cool, and store in an airtight container.

Nutrition Facts

Per Serving:

80.2 calories; protein 0.8g 2% DV; carbohydrates 9.9g 3% DV; fat 4.3g 7% DV; cholesterol 15mg 5% DV; sodium 58.8mg 2% DV.

Snowballs

Prep: 15 mins **Cook:** 5 mins **Total:** 20 mins **Servings:** 24 **Yield:** 24 snowballs

Ingredients

- 1 cup 2% milk
- 1 cup white sugar
- ¼ cup butter
- ¼ cup unsweetened cocoa powder
- 2 teaspoons vanilla extract
- 2 cups rolled oats
- 2 ½ cups unsweetened shredded coconut, divided

Directions

Step 1

Combine milk, sugar, butter, and cocoa powder in a large pot; bring to a boil for 3 minutes. Stir vanilla extract into the milk mixture; boil another 2 minutes. Remove pot from heat.

Step 2

Stir oats and 2 cups coconut into the milk mixture until thoroughly mixed; cool for 5 minutes.

Step 3

Spread 1/2 cup coconut onto a plate. Roll the mixture into 24 balls and roll in the coconut. Set on a sheet of parchment paper until finished.

Nutrition Facts

Per Serving:

146.9 calories; protein 2.1g 4% DV; carbohydrates 16.2g 5% DV; fat 8.9g 14% DV; cholesterol 5.9mg 2% DV; sodium 22mg 1% DV.

Mom's Peanut Butter Blossom Cookies

Prep: 15 mins **Cook:** 10 mins **Additional:** 30 mins **Total:** 55 mins **Servings:** 48 **Yield:** 4 dozen cookies

Ingredients

- ¾ cup peanut butter
- ½ cup shortening
- ⅓ cup white sugar
- ⅓ cup light brown sugar
- 1 egg
- 2 tablespoons milk
- 1 teaspoon vanilla extract

- 1 ½ cups all-purpose flour
- 1 teaspoon baking soda
- ½ teaspoon salt
- 1 (8 ounce) package milk chocolate candy kisses (such as Hershey's Kisses®), unwrapped

Directions

Step 1

Preheat oven to 375 degrees F (190 degrees C).

Step 2

Beat peanut butter and shortening together in a bowl using an electric mixer until smooth and creamy; add white sugar and brown sugar and beat until fluffy. Add egg, milk, and vanilla extract to creamed mixture and beat until smooth.

Step 3

Mix flour, baking soda, and salt together in a separate bowl; gradually beat into the creamed mixture until dough is just mixed. Shape dough into 1-inch balls and arrange on a baking sheet.

Step 4

Bake in the preheated oven until cookies are lightly browned, 8 to 10 minutes. Immediately press a chocolate kiss into the center of each cookie. Transfer cookies to a wire rack to cool.

Nutrition Facts

Per Serving:

94.3 calories; protein 1.9g 4% DV; carbohydrates 9.5g 3% DV; fat 5.8g 9% DV; cholesterol 5mg 2% DV; sodium 75.1mg 3% DV.

Chocolate Spritz (Cookie Press)

Prep: 15 mins **Cook:** 10 mins **Total:** 25 mins **Servings:** 84 **Yield:** 84 cookies

Ingredients

- 1 ½ cups butter, softened
- 1 cup white sugar
- ¼ cup unsweetened cocoa powder
- 1 teaspoon baking powder

- 1 egg
- 1 teaspoon vanilla extract
- 3 ¼ cups all-purpose flour

Directions

Step 1

Preheat oven to 375 degrees F (190 degrees C).

Step 2

Beat butter in a large mixing bowl using an electric mixer until creamy; add sugar, cocoa powder, and baking powder. Beat until combined. Scrape sides of bowl down if needed. Stir egg and vanilla extract into butter mixture until just combined; mix in flour.

Step 3

Fill the cookie press with dough; press cookies onto an ungreased baking sheet.

Step 4

Bake in the preheated oven until edges of cookies are lightly browned, 8 to 10 minutes.

Nutrition Facts

Per Serving:

57.5 calories; protein 0.7g 1% DV; carbohydrates 6.2g 2% DV; fat 3.4g 5% DV; cholesterol 10.9mg 4% DV; sodium 30.1mg 1% DV.

Ricciarelli

Prep: 40 mins **Cook:** 7 mins **Additional:** 13 hrs **Total:** 13 hrs 47 mins **Servings:** 20 **Yield:** 20 cookies

Ingredients

- 2 ¼ cups white sugar
- 2 cups blanched almonds
- ½ cup egg whites
- 1 drop vanilla extract
- ¼ cup confectioners' sugar, or as needed
- 2 tablespoons all-purpose flour

Directions

Step 1

Combine white sugar and almonds in the bowl of a food processor; pulse into a fine powder. Pour into a bowl.

Step 2

Combine 1/4 cup egg whites and vanilla extract in a bowl; add to almond-sugar mixture, mixing as little as possible. Wrap dough in plastic wrap and refrigerate for 12 hours.

Step 3

Line a baking sheet with parchment paper.

Step 4

Remove dough from fridge. Sift 2 tablespoons confectioners' sugar and flour onto a clean work surface. Place dough in the center and add remaining 1/4 cup egg whites. Knead egg whites into dough until soft and smooth, adding additional confectioners' sugar and flour as needed.

Step 5

Roll portions of dough into 1-inch-thick logs. Take walnut-sized dough pieces from each log and shape into diamonds with slightly wet hands. Place cookies on the prepared baking sheet and generously dust with confectioner's sugar. Let rest at room temperature for 1 to 2 hours.

Step 6

Preheat oven to 350 degrees F (175 degrees C).

Step 7

Bake cookies in the preheated oven until lightly golden, 7 to 8 minutes. Cool on the baking sheet before serving.

Nutrition Facts

Per Serving:

183.3 calories; protein 3.9g 8% DV; carbohydrates 27.6g 9% DV; fat 7.3g 11% DV; cholesterolmg; sodium 14.2mg 1% DV.

Lebkuchen II

Servings: 84 **Yield:** 14 dozen

Ingredients

- 3 cups honey
- 2 ¼ cups packed brown sugar
- 3 large eggs eggs
- 1 tablespoon lemon zest
- 3 tablespoons lemon juice
- 8 ¼ cups all-purpose flour
- 1 ½ teaspoons baking soda
- 1 tablespoon ground cinnamon
- 1 ½ teaspoons ground allspice

- 1 ½ teaspoons ground nutmeg
- 1 teaspoon ground cloves
- 1 cup chopped candied citron
- 1 cup chopped pecans
- 2 cups sliced almonds
- 1 ½ cups white sugar
- ¾ cup water
- ⅓ cup sifted confectioners' sugar

Directions

Step 1

Bring honey to a boil in a large Dutch oven; remove from heat, and cool slightly. Stir in brown sugar, beaten eggs, lemon rind, and juice.

Step 2

Combine flour, baking soda, and spices in a large mixing bowl; gradually add to honey mixture, stirring well. Stir in citron and chopped pecans, blending well. Cover and chill overnight.

Step 3

Preheat oven to 400 degrees F (200 degrees C).

Step 4

Shape dough into 1-inch balls; place 2 inches apart on greased cookie sheets. Gently press ball to 1/4-inch thickness with bottom of a glass dipped in cool water. Gently press an almond slice in the center of each cookie. Bake for about 10 minutes. Remove cookie sheets from oven. Brush glaze over cookies and remove to wire racks to cool.

151

Step 5

To Make Glaze: Combine 1 1/2 cups sugar and water in a small heavy saucepan; cook over low heat, stirring until sugar dissolves. Cook over high heat, without stirring, until mixture reaches thread stage (230 degrees F). Remove from heat; stir in confectioners' sugar, mixing well. Place over low heat, if necessary, to maintain basting consistency.

Nutrition Facts

Per Serving:

154.5 calories; protein 2.1g 4% DV; carbohydrates 32.3g 10% DV; fat 2.4g 4% DV; cholesterol 6.6mg 2% DV; sodium 35.8mg 1% DV.

Springerle V

Servings: 60 **Yield:** 4 to 5 dozen

Ingredients

- 4 large eggs eggs
- 1 pound confectioners' sugar
- 2 teaspoons anise extract

- 4 ¼ cups sifted all-purpose flour
- 2 teaspoons baking powder

Directions

Step 1

In a large bowl, beat eggs until light with an electric mixer on high speed. Reduce speed and add the anise extract and confectioners' sugar. Continue beating at medium speed until well combined. Sift together the flour and baking powder; stir into the egg mixture, dough will be quite stiff.

Step 2

Roll out dough to 3/8 inch thickness. Imprint with a springerle board and cut apart. Place cookies onto a cookie sheet and let rest uncovered overnight.

Step 3

Preheat oven to 350 degrees F (175 degrees C). Bake cookies for 7 to 10 minutes.

Nutrition Facts

Per Serving:

66.8 calories; protein 1.3g 3% DV; carbohydrates 14.4g 5% DV; fat 0.4g 1% DV; cholesterol 12.4mg 4% DV; sodium 21.2mg 1% DV.

White Chocolate Thumbprint Cookies

Prep: 20 mins **Cook:** 20 mins **Additional:** 1 hr 5 mins **Total:** 1 hr 45 mins **Servings:** 72 **Yield:** 6 dozen cookies

Ingredients

- 1 pound butter, softened
- 1 ½ cups white sugar
- 1 teaspoon vanilla extract
- 4 cups all-purpose flour
- 2 teaspoons baking powder
- 1 cup chopped walnuts
- 1 (8 ounce) jar seedless raspberry jam
- 3 (1.55 ounce) bars white chocolate, chopped
- 1 tablespoon vegetable shortening

Directions

Step 1

Beat butter, sugar, and vanilla extract together in a bowl until creamy and smooth. Mix flour and baking powder together in a separate bowl; gradually beat flour mixture into creamed butter mixture until dough is smooth. Fold walnuts into the dough. Refrigerate dough for 1 hour.

Step 2

Preheat oven to 325 degrees F (165 degrees C).

Step 3

Roll cookie dough into 6 dozen small balls and place them 2 inches apart on a baking sheet. Press the center of each ball using your thumb to form a small well. Fill the depressions with jam.

Step 4

Bake in the preheated oven until cookies are light golden brown, about 18 minutes.

Step 5

Melt white chocolate and shortening together in the top of a double boiler over simmering water, stirring frequently and scraping down the sides with a rubber spatula to avoid scorching. Drizzle melted white chocolate mixture over cookies.

Step 6

Cool cookies on the sheet for 5 minutes before removing to cool completely on a wire rack.

Nutrition Facts

Per Serving:

116.7 calories; protein 1.1g 2% DV; carbohydrates 12.8g 4% DV; fat 7g 11% DV; cholesterol 13.9mg 5% DV; sodium 51.7mg 2% DV.

Mom's Sugar Cookies

Prep: 30 mins **Cook:** 15 mins **Additional:** 3 hrs **Total:** 3 hrs 45 mins **Servings:** 60 **Yield:** 60 cookies

Ingredients

- 1 cup butter, softened
- 1 egg
- 1 teaspoon pure vanilla extract
- ½ teaspoon almond extract
- 1 ½ cups confectioners' sugar
- 2 ½ cups all-purpose flour
- 1 teaspoon baking soda
- 1 teaspoon cream of tartar

Directions

Step 1

Beat butter, egg, vanilla extract, and almond extract together in a bowl using an electric mixer until smooth. Add confectioners' sugar and beat until incorporated. Mix flour, baking soda, and cream of tartar into butter mixture until dough sticks together. Cover bowl with plastic wrap and refrigerate for at least 3 hours.

Step 2

Preheat oven to 375 degrees F (190 degrees C). Lightly grease baking sheets.

Step 3

Cut dough into quarters and roll each quarter onto a floured work surface to almost 1/4-inch thickness. Cut dough into shapes using cookie cutters and arrange on the prepared baking sheets.

Step 4

Bake each batch in the preheated oven until edges start to brown, about 8 minutes.

Nutrition Facts

Per Serving:

59.9 calories; protein 0.7g 1% DV; carbohydrates 7.1g 2% DV; fat 3.2g 5% DV; cholesterol 11.2mg 4% DV; sodium 44.1mg 2% DV.

Gingerbread Man Cookies

Prep: 30 mins **Cook:** 10 mins **Additional:** 1 day **Total:** 1 day **Servings:** 48 **Yield:** 4 dozen

Ingredients

- 3 ½ cups all-purpose flour
- 1 ½ teaspoons ground ginger
- 1 ½ teaspoons ground cinnamon
- ¼ teaspoon salt
- ½ cup shortening
- ½ cup white sugar

- 1 egg
- 1 cup molasses
- 1 teaspoon baking soda
- 1 ½ teaspoons warm water
- ¼ cup raisins for decorating

Directions

Step 1

Combine flour, ginger, cinnamon, and salt in a bowl and set aside.

Step 2

In large bowl, cream shortening and sugar until smooth. Mix in egg and molasses. Dissolve baking soda in 1 1/2 teaspoons warm water and add to egg mixture; stir until combined.

Step 3

Mix in dry ingredients well blended. Shape dough into a disk, wrap in plastic, and refrigerate overnight.

Step 4

Preheat oven to 350 degrees F. Grease cookie sheets or line them with parchment paper.

Step 5

Lightly flour a work surface. Roll out dough to a thickness of 1/4 inch. Cut out gingerbread men using cookie cutters and place 2 inches apart on cookie sheets. Use raisins to make eyes, noses and buttons.

Step 6

Bake in the preheated oven, or until firm, 10 to 12 minutes. Let cool on wire racks.

Nutrition Facts

Per Serving:

84.1 calories; protein 1.1g 2% DV; carbohydrates 14.8g 5% DV; fat 2.3g 4% DV; cholesterol 3.9mg 1% DV; sodium 42.6mg 2% DV.

Almond Meringue Cookies

Prep: 15 mins **Cook:** 15 mins **Total:** 30 mins **Servings:** 36 **Yield:** 3 dozen

Ingredients

- 11 ounces ground almonds
- 3 large egg whites egg whites
- 1 cup confectioners' sugar
- 1 teaspoon grated lemon zest
- ¾ teaspoon ground cinnamon

Directions

Step 1

Preheat the oven to 325 degrees F (165 degrees C). Grease and lightly flour cookie sheets.

Step 2

In a large bowl, whip egg whites until soft peaks form. Gradually sprinkle in the sugar and keep whipping until the egg whites can hold a stiff peak, this will take about 5 minutes. Set aside about 1/2 cup of the egg whites. Add the lemon zest and cinnamon to the rest of the meringue, and fold in the almonds until everything is evenly blended.

Step 3

Drop mounds by spoonfuls onto the prepared baking sheets. Top each cookie with a smaller dollop of the reserved meringue.

Step 4

Bake for 15 minutes in the preheated oven, until golden brown. Remove cookies from the baking sheets to cool on wire racks.

Nutrition Facts

Per Serving:

66.3 calories; protein 2g 4% DV; carbohydrates 5.5g 2% DV; fat 4.5g 7% DV; cholesterolmg; sodium 5.2mg.

Bon Bon Christmas Cookies

Servings: 24 **Yield:** 2 dozen

Ingredients

- ½ (8 ounce) package cream cheese
- ½ cup butter flavored shortening
- 2 cups sifted all-purpose flour
- 1 ½ cups sifted confectioners' sugar
- 2 (10 ounce) jars maraschino cherries, drained

Directions

Step 1

In a medium bowl, stir together the shortening and cream cheese until well blended. Stir in the flour, you may need to use your hands to help it form a dough. If the mixture seems too dry, add a couple of teaspoons of water. Cover and chill several hours or overnight.

Step 2

Preheat the oven to 375 degrees F (190 degrees C). Lightly grease cookie sheets.

Step 3

Before rolling out the dough, dust the rolling surface heavily with confectioners' sugar. Roll the dough out to 1/8 inch thickness. Cut into 1x4 inch strips. Place a cherry on the end of each strip. Roll up each strip starting with the cherry. Place on prepared cookie sheets and dust with a little of the confectioners' sugar.

Step 4

Bake for 7 to 10 minutes in the preheated oven. Cookies should brown slightly. Dust again with the confectioners' sugar. Allow cookies to cool before serving, the cherries are very hot!

Nutrition Facts

Per Serving:

151.2 calories; protein 1.5g 3% DV; carbohydrates 22.7g 7% DV; fat 6.2g 10% DV; cholesterol 5.1mg 2% DV; sodium 14.3mg 1% DV.

Holly Christmas Cookies

Prep: 15 mins **Cook:** 10 mins **Additional:** 1 hr **Total:** 1 hr 25 mins **Servings:** 18 **Yield:** 3 dozen

Ingredients

- 1 (16 ounce) package large marshmallows
- ½ cup butter, softened
- 1 ½ teaspoons vanilla extract
- 1 ½ teaspoons green food coloring
- 4 ½ cups cornflakes cereal
- 1 (2.25 ounce) package cinnamon red hot candies

Directions

Step 1

In a saucepan over low heat, melt together the marshmallows, butter, vanilla, and food coloring. Mix in the cornflakes cereal.

Step 2

Drop by spoonfuls on wax paper, and decorate with red hots. Set aside, and allow to cool.

Nutrition Facts

Per Serving:

164.5 calories; protein 1g 2% DV; carbohydrates 29.8g 10% DV; fat 5.2g 8% DV; cholesterol 13.6mg 5% DV; sodium 108.2mg 4% DV.

Rum Balls I

Servings: 36 **Yield:** 36 balls

Ingredients

- 3 cups vanilla wafer crumbs
- ½ cup ground pecans
- 3 tablespoons cocoa
- 1 cup confectioners' sugar
- 3 tablespoons light corn syrup
- ⅓ cup water
- 2 teaspoons rum flavored extract
- ¼ cup confectioners' sugar

Directions

Step 1

In a medium bowl, mix vanilla wafer crumbs, ground pecans, cocoa, 1 cup confectioners' sugar, corn syrup, water, and rum flavoring together.

Step 2

Roll mixture into 1 inch balls, and then roll in remaining confectioners' sugar. Store, covered, about a week before serving.

Nutrition Facts

Per Serving:

101.6 calories; protein 0.8g 2% DV; carbohydrates 16.5g 5% DV; fat 3.8g 6% DV; cholesterolmg; sodium 47.1mg 2% DV.

Chewy Noels

Prep: 15 mins **Cook:** 20 mins **Total:** 35 mins **Servings:** 18 **Yield:** 1 1/2 dozen

Ingredients

- 2 tablespoons butter
- 1 cup packed brown sugar
- 5 tablespoons all-purpose flour
- ⅛ teaspoon baking soda
- 2 large eggs eggs, beaten
- 1 teaspoon vanilla extract
- 1 cup chopped walnuts
- ¼ cup confectioners' sugar for dusting

Directions

Step 1

Preheat oven to 350 degrees F (175 degrees C). Melt the butter in a 7x11 inch baking dish, and tilt the pan to coat all of the sides; set aside.

Step 2

In a medium bowl, stir together the brown sugar, flour, and baking soda. Mix in the eggs and vanilla until smooth, then stir in the walnuts. Pour over the melted butter.

Step 3

Bake in the preheated oven for 20 minutes, or until the edges begin to brown. Cool, then cut into squares, and dust with confectioners sugar.

Nutrition Facts

123.6 calories; protein 1.9g 4% DV; carbohydrates 16.3g 5% DV; fat 6.1g 9% DV; cholesterol 24.1mg 8% DV; sodium 29.2mg 1% DV.

Coconut Rum Balls

Servings: 4 **Yield:** 4 to 5 servings

Ingredients

- 1 (12 ounce) package vanilla wafers, crushed
- 1 ⅓ cups flaked coconut
- 1 cup finely chopped walnuts

- 1 (14 ounce) can sweetened condensed milk
- ¼ cup rum
- ⅛ cup confectioners' sugar

Directions

Step 1

In a large bowl, combine crumbs, coconut, & nuts. Add sweetened condensed milk & rum; mix well. Chill 4 hours.

Step 2

Shape into 1- inch balls. Roll in sugar. Store in covered container in refrigerator 24 hours before serving.

Nutrition Facts

Per Serving:

1063 calories; protein 16.6g 33% DV; carbohydrates 133.7g 43% DV; fat 50.8g 78% DV; cholesterol 33.3mg 11% DV; sodium 452.6mg 18% DV.

Tyler's Raspberry Thumbprints with White Chocolate Glaze

Prep: 20 mins **Cook:** 15 mins **Additional:** 10 mins **Total:** 45 mins **Servings:** 48 **Yield:** 4 dozen

Ingredients

- ½ cup butter, softened
- ½ cup sour cream
- 1 cup white sugar
- 2 tablespoons milk

- 2 large eggs eggs
- 2 ⅔ cups all-purpose flour
- 2 cups rolled oats
- 1 teaspoon baking soda

- 5 ounces white chocolate, chopped
- ⅔ cup raspberry preserves
- 1 tablespoon butter
- ½ (1 ounce) square white chocolate
- 1 cup confectioners' sugar
- 2 tablespoons milk

Directions

Step 1

Preheat oven to 350 degrees F (175 degrees C).

Step 2

In a large bowl, cream together the 1/2 cup butter and sugar until smooth. Blend in the sour cream, 2 tablespoons of milk and eggs. Combine the flour, oats and baking soda, gradually stir into the creamed mixture. Finally, stir in the chopped white chocolate. Drop by rounded spoonfuls onto the prepared cookie sheet. Using a finger or your thumb, press a dent into the center of each cookie. Fill the dent with a 1/2 teaspoon of raspberry preserves.

Step 3

Bake for 8 to 10 minutes in the preheated oven. Allow cookies to cool on baking sheet for 5 minutes before removing to a wire rack to cool completely.

Step 4

To make the glaze: Combine 1 tablespoon butter and 1/2 ounce white chocolate in a microwave safe bowl. cook on high, stirring every 15 seconds until smooth. Gradually beat in the confectioners' sugar and milk until icing is of a drizzling consistency. Drizzle over cooled cookies.

Nutrition Facts

Per Serving:

122 calories; protein 1.8g 4% DV; carbohydrates 19.3g 6% DV; fat 4.3g 7% DV; cholesterol 16.4mg 6% DV; sodium 49.7mg 2% DV.

Gingerbread People from JELL-O

Prep: 20 mins **Cook:** 10 mins **Additional:** 1 hr **Total:** 1 hr 30 mins **Servings:** 20 **Yield:** 20 cookies

Ingredients

- ¾ cup butter, softened
- ¾ cup packed brown sugar
- 1 (3.4 ounce) package JELL-O Butterscotch Instant Pudding
- 1 egg
- 2 cups flour
- 1 teaspoon baking soda
- 1 tablespoon ground ginger

- 1 ½ teaspoons ground cinnamon

Directions

Step 1

Beat butter, sugar, dry pudding mix and egg in large bowl with mixer until well blended. Mix remaining ingredients. Gradually add to butter mixture, beating well after each addition. Refrigerate 1 hour or until firm.

Step 2

Heat oven to 350 degrees F. Roll out dough on lightly floured surface to 1/4-inch thickness; cut into gingerbread shapes with 4-inch cookie cutter, re-rolling trimmings. Place, 2 inches apart, on baking sheets sprayed with cooking spray. Use straw to make hole near top of each cutout.

Step 3

Bake 10 to 12 min. or until edges are lightly browned. Cool on baking sheets 3 min. Remove to wire racks; cool completely. Decorate as desired. Insert ribbon through holes to hang cookies on tree.

Nutrition Facts

Per Serving:

160.1 calories; protein 1.7g 3% DV; carbohydrates 22.4g 7% DV; fat 7.3g 11% DV; cholesterol 27.6mg 9% DV; sodium 194.9mg 8% DV.

Anise Drops

Servings: 36 **Yield:** 2 -3 dozen

Ingredients

- 3 large eggs eggs, beaten
- 1 cup white sugar
- 2 cups all-purpose flour
- ½ teaspoon baking powder
- ½ teaspoon cream of tartar
- 1 tablespoon anise seed

Directions

Step 1

Preheat oven to 350 degrees F (175 degrees C).

162

Step 2

Combine the sugar and the beaten eggs and continue to beat for 15 minutes. Stir in the flour, baking powder, cream of tartar and the anise seeds.

Step 3

Drop by teaspoonfuls onto a greased cookie sheet and bake at 350 degrees F (175 degrees C) for 15 minutes.

Nutrition Facts

Per Serving:

53.5 calories; protein 1.3g 3% DV; carbohydrates 11g 4% DV; fat 0.5g 1% DV; cholesterol 15.5mg 5% DV; sodium 12.8mg 1% DV.

Pfeffernuesse IV

Prep: 20 mins **Cook:** 12 mins **Additional:** 4 hrs 28 mins **Total:** 5 hrs **Servings:** 60 **Yield:** 5 dozen

Ingredients

- 4 cups all-purpose flour
- ½ cup white sugar
- 1 ¼ teaspoons baking soda
- 1 ½ teaspoons ground cinnamon
- 1 teaspoon ground cloves
- 1 teaspoon ground nutmeg
- ½ teaspoon ground allspice
- 1 dash ground black pepper
- ¾ cup molasses
- ½ cup butter
- 2 large eggs eggs, beaten
- 1 ½ cups confectioners' sugar

Directions

Step 1

In a large bowl, stir together the flour, sugar, baking soda, cinnamon, cloves, nutmeg and allspice. In a medium saucepan over medium heat, combine molasses and butter. Heat, stirring occasionally, until the butter is melted. Remove from heat and allow to cool to room temperature. When the mixture has cooled, beat in the eggs. Blend the molasses mixture into the dry ingredients until evenly mixed. Cover and refrigerate for at least 3 to 4 hours.

Step 2

Preheat oven to 350 degrees F (175 degrees C). Grease cookie sheets. Roll dough into 1 inch balls and place them 2 inches apart onto the cookie sheets.

Step 3

Bake for 12 to 14 minutes in the preheated oven, or until firm. While cookies are still warm, toss them in a bag with confectioners' sugar and toss to coat. When cool, toss with sugar again.

Nutrition Facts

Per Serving:

76.9 calories; protein 1.1g 2% DV; carbohydrates 14.2g 5% DV; fat 1.8g 3% DV; cholesterol 10.3mg 3% DV; sodium 41.3mg 2% DV.

Chocolate Covered Orange Balls

Servings: 18 Yield: 3 dozen

Ingredients

- 1 pound confectioners' sugar
- 1 (12 ounce) package vanilla wafers, crushed
- 1 cup chopped walnuts
- ¼ pound butter
- 1 (6 ounce) can frozen orange juice concentrate, thawed
- 1 ½ pounds milk chocolate, melted

Directions

Step 1

In a large bowl, combine the confectioners sugar, vanilla wafers, walnuts, butter and orange juice. Mix well and shape into 1 inch round balls; allow to dry for 1 hour.

Step 2

Place chocolate chips in top of double boiler. Stir frequently over medium heat until melted.

Step 3

Dip balls into melted chocolate and place in decorative paper cups.

Nutrition Facts

Per Serving:

495.4 calories; protein 5g 10% DV; carbohydrates 66.3g 21% DV; fat 24.2g 37% DV; cholesterol 22.3mg 7% DV; sodium 124.1mg 5% DV.

Amaretti Italian Cookies

Prep: 15 mins **Cook:** 15 mins **Total:** 30 mins **Servings:** 45 **Yield:** 45 cookies

Ingredients

- 5 cups finely chopped roasted almonds
- 2 cups white sugar
- 1 ½ teaspoons unsweetened cocoa powder
- 4 large eggs eggs
- 1 (1 ounce) bottle almond extract, or to taste
- ¼ cup white sugar
- 45 almonds whole almonds

Directions

Step 1

Preheat oven to 350 degrees F (175 degrees C). Line 2 baking sheets with parchment paper.

Step 2

Mix chopped almonds, 2 cups white sugar, and cocoa powder together in a bowl; add eggs and almond extract and stir until batter is well mixed. Form teaspoonfuls of batter into small balls.

Step 3

Place 1/4 cup sugar in a bowl and roll balls in the sugar. Press a finger into the center of each ball, making an indentation. Place 1 almond in each indentation. Arrange cookies 2 inches apart on the baking sheets.

Step 4

Bake in the preheated oven until edges begin to crisp, about 15 minutes.

Nutrition Facts

Per Serving:

145.4 calories; protein 4.2g 8% DV; carbohydrates 13.3g 4% DV; fat 9.2g 14% DV; cholesterol 16.5mg 6% DV; sodium 6.4mg.

Cherry-Almond Icebox Cookies

Prep: 15 mins **Cook:** 20 mins **Additional:** 30 mins **Total:** 1 hr 5 mins **Servings:** 24 **Yield:** 24 bars

Ingredients

- 1 cup butter, softened
- 1 cup brown sugar
- 2 cups all-purpose flour
- ½ cup sliced blanched almonds
- ½ cup chopped red candied cherries
- 2 ounces white chocolate

Directions

Step 1

Preheat oven to 350 degrees F (175 degrees C). Line bottom and sides of an 11x7-inch glass baking pan with parchment paper; leave paper hanging over pan edges so that cookies can be lifted out after baking.

Step 2

Beat butter and brown sugar together with an electric mixer until light and fluffy, about 2 minutes. Stir flour into butter mixture until crumbly; stir in almonds and cherries. Press mixture evenly into the bottom of prepared pan.

Step 3

Bake in the preheated oven until lightly golden at edges, about 20 minutes. Score with a sharp knife into bars while in the pan and still warm; allow cookies to cool about 30 minutes. Lift cookies from pan and slice to separate along scored marks.

Step 4

Melt white chocolate in a microwave-safe glass or ceramic bowl in 30-second intervals, stirring after each melting, for 1 to 3 minutes (depending on your microwave). Do not overheat or chocolate will scorch. Drizzle melted white chocolate over cookies or dip half of each cookie into melted white chocolate.

Nutrition Facts

Per Serving:

175.2 calories; protein 1.8g 4% DV; carbohydrates 21g 7% DV; fat 9.7g 15% DV; cholesterol 20.8mg 7% DV; sodium 62.2mg 3% DV.

Cherry Bell Cookies

Servings: 30 Yield: 5 dozen

Ingredients

- 3 cups all-purpose flour
- ½ teaspoon baking soda
- ½ teaspoon salt
- 1 teaspoon ground ginger
- ½ teaspoon instant coffee granules
- 1 cup butter
- 1 ¼ cups packed brown sugar
- ¼ cup dark corn syrup
- 1 egg, beaten
- 1 tablespoon cream
- ⅓ cup packed brown sugar
- 1 tablespoon butter
- 3 tablespoons cherry juice
- 1 ½ cups chopped walnuts
- 60 cherries maraschino cherries, halved

Directions

Step 1

Sift together: 3 cups flour, 1/2 teaspoon baking soda, 1/2 teaspoon salt, 1 teaspoon ginger and 1/2 teaspoon instant coffee. Put aside.

Step 2

Cream 1 cup butter or margarine. Add 1 1/4 cups brown sugar. Cream well. Blend in dark corn syrup, egg, and cream. Add dry ingredients and mix well.

Step 3

Roll out dough, 1/3 at a time on floured board to 1/8 inch thickness. Cut cookies into 2 1/2 inch rounds. Place on ungreased cookie sheet.

Step 4

To Make Filling: Combine 1/3 firmly packed brown sugar, 1 tablespoon butter, 3 tablespoons cherry juice. Stir in 1 1/2 cups chopped nuts, chopped fine.

Step 5

Place 1/2 teaspoon filling in center of each round. Shape into a bell by folding sides of dough to meet over the filling using spatula to fold over sides. Make top of bell narrower than at the clapper end. Place 1/2 of a maraschino cherry (cut side down) at open end of each bell for clapper. Bake at 350 degrees F for 12-15 minutes.

Nutrition Facts

Per Serving:

214.2 calories; protein 2.5g 5% DV; carbohydrates 28.1g 9% DV; fat 10.8g 17% DV; cholesterol 24.2mg 8% DV; sodium 116.8mg 5% DV.

Peanut Butter Christmas Mice

Prep: 30 mins **Cook:** 10 mins **Additional:** 1 hr **Total:** 1 hr 40 mins **Servings:** 60 **Yield:** 60 cookies

Ingredients

- ½ cup butter, room temperature
- 1 cup creamy peanut butter
- ½ cup packed light brown sugar
- ½ cup white sugar
- 1 egg
- 1 teaspoon vanilla extract
- ½ teaspoon baking soda
- 1 ½ cups all-purpose flour
- 1 cup peanut halves
- ¼ cup green candy sprinkles
- 60 piece (blank)s 3-inch pieces red shoestring licorice

Directions

Step 1

In a large bowl combine butter and peanut butter; beat until creamy. Add brown and white sugar and beat until fluffy. Beat in egg, vanilla extract and baking soda until well blended. With mixer on low, mix in flour just until blended. Cover and chill for 1 hour, or until firm.

Step 2

Preheat oven to 350 degrees F (175 degrees C).

Step 3

Shape 1 level tablespoon of dough into 1 inch balls. Taper each ball at one end into a teardrop shape. Press flat on one side. Place flat sides down, 2 inches apart on ungreased cookie sheets. Press the sides of the dough in to raise the 'backs' of the mice, as dough will spread slightly during baking.

Step 4

Gently push 2 peanut halves in each 'mouse' for ears, and 2 pieces of green candy for eyes. With a toothpick make a hole 1/2 inch deep in the tail ends.

Step 5

Bake in preheated oven for 8 to 10 minutes, or until firm.

Step 6

Transfer to a cooling rack and insert licorice pieces as tails.

Nutrition Facts

Per Serving:

118.2 calories; protein 2.4g 5% DV; carbohydrates 16.3g 5% DV; fat 5.2g 8% DV; cholesterol 7.2mg 2% DV; sodium 48.1mg 2% DV.

Basic Gingersnap Cookies

Prep: 15 mins **Cook:** 8 mins **Additional:** 1 hr 30 mins **Total:** 1 hr 53 mins **Servings:** 36 **Yield:** 6 dozen cookies

Ingredients

- 6 cups all-purpose flour
- 1 teaspoon baking soda
- ½ teaspoon baking powder
- 1 ½ teaspoons salt

- 4 teaspoons ground ginger
- 4 teaspoons ground cinnamon
- 1 ½ teaspoons ground cloves
- 1 teaspoon ground black pepper
- 1 cup unsalted butter, softened
- 1 cup packed brown sugar
- 2 large eggs eggs
- 1 cup unsulfured molasses

Directions

Step 1

Sift together the flour, baking soda, baking powder, salt, ginger, cinnamon, cloves, and black pepper; set aside. In a large bowl, or stand mixer with the paddle attachment, cream together the butter and sugar until smooth. Beat in the eggs one at a time, then stir in the molasses. Gradually mix in the sifted ingredients. Divide the dough into thirds and wrap in plastic wrap. Refrigerate for at least one hour.

Step 2

Preheat oven to 350 degrees F (175 degrees C).

Step 3

On a lightly floured surface, roll the dough out to 1/8 inch in thickness. Cut into desired shapes with cookie cutters. Place cookies 1 1/2 inches apart onto cookie sheets.

Step 4

Bake for 8 to 10 minutes in the preheated oven, until cookies are crisp but not dark. Remove to wire racks to cool completely. Decorate as desired.

Nutrition Facts

Per Serving:

176.4 calories; protein 2.6g 5% DV; carbohydrates 29.2g 9% DV; fat 5.6g 9% DV; cholesterol 23.9mg 8% DV; sodium 147.3mg 6% DV.

Rum Sugar Cookies

Prep: 20 mins **Cook:** 9 mins **Additional:** 2 hrs 1 min **Total:** 2 hrs 30 mins **Servings:** 48 **Yield:** 4 dozen

Ingredients

- 3 cups all-purpose flour
- ½ teaspoon baking soda
- ½ teaspoon salt
- ½ teaspoon baking powder
- 1 cup butter
- 2 large eggs eggs
- 1 cup white sugar
- 1 teaspoon rum flavored extract
- ½ teaspoon almond extract
- ⅛ teaspoon ground nutmeg

Directions

Step 1

Mix together flour, baking soda, salt, baking powder, and butter until the mixture resembles cornmeal.

Step 2

Combine eggs, sugar, rum extract, almond extract, and nutmeg until well mixed. Pour the egg mixture into the flour mixture. Stir until well blended. Divide the dough into two equal halves. Refrigerate the dough for 2 hours.

Step 3

Preheat the oven to 350 degrees F (175 degrees C).

Step 4

Place dough on a lightly floured surface. Roll the dough out until it is 1/8 inch thick. Using a cookie cutter cut the dough into cookies (whatever shapes you please). Place the cookies on an ungreased baking sheet.

Step 5

Bake in the preheated oven until the edges are golden, 7 to 9 minutes. Allow the cookies to cool on the baking sheet for 1 minute before removing to a wire rack to cool completely.

Nutrition Facts

Per Serving:

81.9 calories; protein 1.1g 2% DV; carbohydrates 10.2g 3% DV; fat 4.1g 6% DV; cholesterol 17.9mg 6% DV; sodium 72.7mg 3% DV.

Tasty Eggnog Cookies

Prep: 15 mins **Cook:** 8 mins **Additional:** 7 mins **Total:** 30 mins **Servings:** 72 **Yield:** 6 dozen

Ingredients

- 1 cup margarine
- 1 cup white sugar
- 1 egg
- 1 cup eggnog
- 3 ¼ cups all-purpose flour

- 1 teaspoon baking powder
- 1 teaspoon baking soda
- ½ teaspoon salt
- 1 ½ cups confectioners' sugar
- 3 tablespoons eggnog

Directions

Step 1

Preheat oven to 350 degrees F (175 degrees C). Grease cookie sheets.

Step 2

In a medium bowl, cream together the margarine and white sugar until smooth. Stir in the egg and 1 cup eggnog. Combine the flour, baking powder, baking soda and salt; stir into the sugar mixture so it is well blended. Drop by rounded spoonfuls onto the prepared cookie sheet. Drop by rounded spoonfuls onto the prepared cookie sheets.

Step 3

Bake for 8 to 10 minutes in the preheated oven. Allow cookies to cool on baking sheet for 5 minutes before removing to a wire rack to cool completely.

Step 4

To prepare the icing, put the confectioners' sugar into a small bowl. Stir in the remaining eggnog one tablespoon at a time until the desired consistency is reached. Spread onto cooled cookies and let dry before serving.

Nutrition Facts

Per Serving:

70 calories; protein 0.9g 2% DV; carbohydrates 10.2g 3% DV; fat 2.9g 5% DV; cholesterol 5.1mg 2% DV; sodium 71.2mg 3% DV.

White Chocolate-Orange-Pistachio Thumbprint Cookies

Prep: 30 mins **Cook:** 10 mins **Additional:** 1 hr **Total:** 1 hr 40 mins **Servings:** 36 **Yield:** 36 cookies

Ingredients

Cookies:

- 1 cup butter, softened
- ¼ cup white sugar
- 2 large egg yolks egg yolks
- ½ teaspoon vanilla extract

- 2 ½ cups all-purpose flour
- ¼ teaspoon salt
- 1 (3.4 ounce) package instant pistachio pudding mix

Filling:

- 2 cups white chocolate chips

- ¼ cup whole milk
- 1 tablespoon grated orange zest
- 2 ounces roasted, salted pistachios, finely chopped

Directions

Step 1

Combine butter, sugar, egg yolks, and vanilla extract in large bowl. Beat using an electric mixer until well mixed. Add flour, salt, and pudding mix; beat well. Chill dough in the refrigerator for 30 minutes.

Step 2

Preheat the oven to 325 degrees F (165 degrees C). Line a baking sheet with parchment paper.

Step 3

Shape dough into 1-inch balls and place on the prepared baking sheets. Make an indentation in the center of each cookie with your thumb.

Step 4

Bake in the preheated oven until lightly golden around the edges, 10 to 12 minutes. Remove from baking sheet and allow to cool on a wire rack, about 30 minutes.

Step 5

Combine white chocolate chips, milk, and orange zest in a microwave-safe bowl. Heat in the microwave for 1 1/2 minutes, stirring every 30 seconds, until chocolate is melted and smooth.

Step 6

Pour white chocolate mixture into a piping bag and pipe into the thumbprint of the cooled cookies. Sprinkle with chopped pistachios.

Nutrition Facts

Per Serving:

162.3 calories; protein 2.2g 4% DV; carbohydrates 16.7g 5% DV; fat 9.8g 15% DV; cholesterol 27.2mg 9% DV; sodium 109.1mg 4% DV.

Fruit and Spice Rounds

Servings: 30 **Yield:** 5 dozen

Ingredients

- 2 cups all-purpose flour
- 1 teaspoon baking soda
- 1 teaspoon salt
- 1 teaspoon ground cinnamon
- ¾ teaspoon ground cloves
- ½ teaspoon ground nutmeg
- 1 cup raisins
- 1 cup dried figs
- 1 cup pitted dates
- ½ cup chopped walnuts
- 1 cup butter
- 1 ½ cups white sugar
- 3 large eggs eggs
- 1 ½ cups sifted confectioners' sugar
- 1 tablespoon butter, softened
- ½ teaspoon vanilla extract
- 5 teaspoons milk

Directions

Step 1

In a food processor or with the fine blade of a food grinder, process or grind raisins, figs, dates and walnuts.

Step 2

In a large mixing bowl beat butter until softened. Add sugar and beat until fluffy. Add eggs and beat well.

Step 3

In a mixing bowl stir together flour, baking soda, salt, cinnamon, cloves, and nutmeg. Add flour mixture and beat until well mixed.

Step 4

Stir in ground fruit mixture. Divide dough in half; cover and chill several hours or overnight.

Step 5

Preheat oven to 375 degrees F. Grease cookie sheet.

Step 6

On a well floured surface roll dough 1/4 inch thick. Cut into rounds with a 2 1/2-inch cookie cutter. Place on cookie sheet and bake for 10-12 minute or until done. Cool on cookie sheet for 2-3 minutes, then remove and cool thoroughly on rack.

Step 7

Combine 1 1/2 cups sifted powdered sugar, 1 tablespoon softened butter or margarine, and 1/2 teaspoon vanilla and enough milk (4-5 tsp) to make icing of drizzling consistency.

Nutrition Facts

Per Serving:

217 calories; protein 2.3g 5% DV; carbohydrates 34.9g 11% DV; fat 8.5g 13% DV; cholesterol 35.9mg 12% DV; sodium 174.6mg 7% DV.

Printed in Great Britain
by Amazon